Pamper Your Possessions

REVISED EDITION

Pamper Your Possessions

BY

Veva Penick Wright

ILLUSTRATIONS BY

Grambs Miller

BARRE PUBLISHING • BARRE, MASSACHUSETTS

Distributed by Crown Publishers, Inc., New York

Inquiries should be addressed to Clarkson N. Potter, Inc., One Park Avenue, New York, N.Y. 10016
Published simultaneously in Canada by
General Publishing Company Limited

Revised edition
Printed in the United States of America

Designed by Katy Homans

Library of Congress Cataloging in Publication Data

Wright, Veva Penick.
  Pamper your possessions.

  1. Antiques—Conservation and restoration.
I. Title.
NK1127.5.W7   1978   745.1   78-10293
ISBN 0-517-53617-X
ISBN 0-517-53524-6 pbk.

Contents

Author's Foreword

TELLING how to protect and care for treasured objects in your home is the service this book will try to render.

Whether an object is antique, old, or modern, the value is there and always will be if you keep it in as nearly perfect condition as possible. Actually, any object begins to deteriorate the moment it leaves the craftman's hands, for time, climate, sun, dryness, humidity, even age encourages the process of deterioration. This is nature's way of reducing all matter to the organic state.

Knowing how to care for things is important and can be exciting knowledge, but what NOT to do is even more important; the DON'TS outweigh the DO'S, and will be emphasized in the following pages.

Though this book in no way attempts to give instructions on restoration of archaeological or museum pieces, or refinishing furniture and *objets d'art*, intensive research has been done on care that can be safely used in the home.

Before turning to instructions on how to care for an object or material, read first the brief history that has been included to introduce each category. Knowledge of the nature and history of your possessions adds a new dimension to your chores; the object cared for becomes a treasure, and you may be encouraged to search even deeper into its origin, development, and history.

Furniture

FURNITURE, whether utilitarian or ornamental, did not just happen; it evolved in design and usability through unknown centuries because of man's insatiable desire for comfort and ornamentation in his surroundings.

The story of furniture unfolds in succeeding civilizations or cultures every hundred or so years. These styles, designated by historians as "Periods" or "Styles" were named for civilizations, cabinetmakers or kings who had been patrons of the arts—some were named for political hierarchies. But periods and styles do not begin or end on a calendar date, as does a century or a year, nor do they abruptly terminate with the death of a monarch for whom the style was named.

The recorded history of furniture begins in Egypt, land of the Pharaohs, 4000 years before the Christian era, primarily because the hot, dry climate of the Nile Valley has preserved in almost perfect condition, priceless relics of the XVIII Dynasty of Egypt; but even more important than the arid climate, was the ancient Egyptian's belief in the immortality of the body as well as the soul. The Pharaohs and the immensely rich, to assure the continuance of their earthly power and golden splendor in the after-life, built enormous tombs in the Valley of the Kings, then stocked them with fabulous furniture and related articles to accompany them on their journey into the unknown.

Through the years many of these tombs have been plundered by thieves but furniture found by archeologists in excavated tombs shows the way of life in Ancient Egypt. Some tombs revealed exquisite miniature villas and toy-like furniture that are perhaps exact replicas of the deceased's earthly environment.

In 1922 archeologists discovered the tomb of the young Egyptian Pharaoh, Tut'Ankhamun. This tomb, situated near Luxor, was virtually undisturbed, and revealed for the first time the true grandeur and craftsmanship of the ancient Egyptian civilization. Rooms were filled with treasures of unsurpassed beauty, but the most priceless item was Tut'-Ankhamun's Throne Chair. This gold chair is one of the great art treasures of the world.

Whether or not the ancient Egyptians copied furniture forms from Babylonian or Assyrian cultures or originated them may never be known, for, unfortunately, history records little of the habits or daily life of prior civilizations. We do know, however, that Egyptian furniture forms and designs have served as models for the civilizations that have followed.

For five or more centuries after the fall of Rome (A.D. 476) Northern tribes—Goths, Danes, Vandals, Vikings, Franks, and others—swept across Europe. Gradually these barbarians settled in the lands they conquered and by the year A.D. 1000 most of the nations of Europe had been established. A European style of architecture and furniture now began to evolve. The art that developed possessed a vigor and strength that was indicative of the character of the barbaric people who created it and led to the development of the Gothic style of the Middle Ages.

The standard of living at this time for both nobility and serf was crude. Furniture was scarce; a chest, a few stools, and a trestle-table sufficed. Furniture in all countries was made by carpenters from thick oak boards, roughly joined. Only the wealthy had bedsteads and beds were little more than boarded boxes surrounded by curtains to secure privacy and keep out the cold; the lowly slept on piles of straw or rushes on the floor. The ordinary seat was a chest, stool or perhaps a bench fixed to the wall.

The original Medieval chair is believed to have evolved by adding a paneled back and sides to a chest. These massive heavily carved chairs were symbols of authority reserved for the master of the house or some distinguished guest. Even royalty rarely had more than two chairs. From this custom evolved the term "Chairman."

This was an age of insecurity and instability. War was endemic in Medieval times. Castles of feudal lords were constantly pillaged, forcing noblemen to move often, taking with them all their possessions. Of necessity, furniture was constructed to be taken apart for transporting. Sturdy, ornamental chests served as trunks for armor, clothes, silver and gold plate, textile hangings, and bedding. These oak chests, either carved or covered in leather, were equipped with handles and locks but rarely had legs, for, there being no roads, trunks had to be transported in wagons or hung in pairs over the backs of sumpter horses.

As culture progressed, other pieces such as cupboards came into use for food storage; a dresser displayed valuable gold and silver plate, and colorful fabrics were draped over benches and stools to add luxury to the austere surroundings.

Early in the 15th century almost all the developing nations of Europe became inspired by the Renaissance of the arts in Italy. The Middle Ages were coming to a close, and there was an awareness of culture and much-needed comfort. Progress in the arts was not confined to architecture, painting, and sculpture. Cabinetmakers of France, Spain, Holland, and later England, stimulated by the Italians, began their own Renaissance. Furniture forms followed the reigning "style", but cabinetmakers in each country accommodated their designs to the climate, temperament, and artistic attitudes of their own people.

Skilled cabinetmakers (ébénistes, in France) visited large centers to learn and improve their techniques, then returned home to teach and work, or migrated to other countries. As a consequence, furniture forms, designs, and techniques were intermingled and widely disseminated throughout Europe and the Colonies.

Our brief story of how furniture evolved must end here, for the subject is beyond the scope of this book. The history of furniture is fascinating: I urge you to pursue it.

WHAT IS AN ANTIQUE

Wood has always been pre-eminent in the construction of furniture, but it must be remembered that wood has its limits of endurance, consequently few examples of early furniture have survived the ravages of time.

If you are interested in buying antiques, it is important to know the meaning of the term, particularly as it is applied to furniture, for the word *antique* is often carelessly used.

Authorities say that a true antique is any "*handcrafted* article made prior to the machine age, approximately 1830." This is the best description I can find, for a machine may be able to cut an exact pattern and produce a copy, but only a craftsman can create an individual piece, and often, it is some small flaw that enhances his work or style and makes the piece more valuable.

Unfortunately, there is now a new Federal law that states, "Any object 100 years old is to be considered an antique," and may be brought into the country duty free. With this new customs law the flood gates are open, and so-called antiques will soon glut the "antiques" marketplace.

Authentic, hand-crafted antiques and signed pieces are rare, for it stands to reason that the few great cabinet-makers and artisans of a hundred and fifty or two hundred years ago could not have produced the volume of antiques on display in dealers' showrooms today. Most of the important pieces are in museums or private collections and not available for purchase at any price.

While searching for antiques, you will find that accredited antique dealers clearly label each piece displayed with a firm price and description: the purchaser is encouraged to thoroughly examine the object, and if desired, another authority will be allowed to verify your findings. If a true antique is purchased a full description should accompany the bill of sale, and if the piece is an import, a copy of the customs' receipt will be presented if it is available.

The National Antique and Art Dealers' Association of America, Inc. is available for consultation and advice. This is a non-profit membership of dealers who have mutually pledged to safeguard the interests of those who buy, sell or collect antiques and works of art. The Association's motto, "Life Devoted to Art," bespeaks the many years of study and experience necessary to acquire the specialized knowledge that has made its members recognized authorities in the various fields of art.

The term *antique* does not necessarily mean that an object is valuable; it merely refers to its age. True value is determined by:

Age

The period it represents

Craftsmanship

Scarcity of such items

If the piece carries the signature of the craftsman and a date, its value skyrockets.

Circa, seen on a tag or mentioned by a dealer, authenticates as nearly as possible, the date or near date the object was made.

Mint Condition is the term used to describe china, porcelain, glass, or breakable *objets d'art* that are in their original condition and have not been repaired. For example, when a complete set of plates, or tea service, is in mint condition, it is far more valuable than if one or more pieces has been repaired, or if a piece is missing.

BEWARE OF FAKED ANTIQUES

Beware! Faked antiques are available in every category of art objects, furniture, pottery, glass, etc. Faked antique furniture is cleverly made by combining old wood with new. The piece is then mutilated even buried for a time, to simulate age and use.

The novice should know that fads create prices and markets for antiques. Often, some well-known decorator sets a trend and the price soars because of demand, as it does with paintings, but these trends can also devaluate the price of other pieces that had previously been in vogue. My best advice is to beware of decorating fads. Choose what pleases you and suits your needs, then remember, the price of any authentic *objet d'art* is what you are willing to pay for it.

HANDCRAFTED REPRODUCTIONS

Handcrafted copies or reasonable facsimiles of period furniture are now available at many price levels. One or two of the well-made reproductions will enhance the beauty of your home, should last a lifetime, and, if cared for, be used and treasured by succeeding generations.

Fine copies of 18th century French furniture have been handcrafted in Paris, in the famous Faubourg St. Antoine, for years. Many of the older pieces are signed by the cabinetmaker.

Handcrafting copies of famous English or American furniture designs is now a flourishing industry in America as well as in Europe, but some of these period reproductions can only be bought through decorators. This is good because you will be advised as to the suitability of a piece in your decorating scheme and be directed to the best outlets.

SELECTING ANTIQUE AND MODERN FURNITURE

When buying furniture, choose each piece with care and don't waste your money. The sensible approach is to seek advice from a top-ranking interior decorator. This advice is usually free, and to your surprise you may find the decorator can supply you with finer quality items for less money. If you prefer to do your own selecting, the decorator will advise and direct you to reliable sources where you can purchase quality merchandise that meets both your budget and your taste.

Visit outstanding antique shops and museums, train your eye to appreciate the best of every furniture period, or style. When you know the style you like, or better still, what you *don't* like, if you can't afford antiques, search for the finest imitations or copies available. Seek out the best furniture companies in your vicinity and when possible obtain entrée to manufacturers' show rooms. Don't eat your heart out for antiques, and don't decorate your rooms with furniture fads seen in the latest magazines—you'll hate yourself for years to come.

When selecting factory-made furniture, don't be ashamed to examine the construction. Some of the most expensive, commercially produced tables, chairs, and sofas are so poorly made they fall apart after a few years' use. Sit in a chair or sofa to evaluate comfort, and always determine the type of "filling" that is used in cushions, back, and armrests of overstuffed items. If cushions are filled with goose down or feathers, the cost will be higher than if foam rubber or dacron has been used. Feather or down cushions have a more luxurious look.

OVERSTUFFED FURNITURE

When planning your decorating scheme, include overstuffed chairs and sofas; they will add comfort and luxury and blend with any style of furniture, whether traditional or modern. These overstuffed classics may be ordered in any size needed, and upholstered or slip-covered in fabrics to blend with any scheme.

Some of the overstuffed favorites are:

Lawson Chair
Lawson Sofa
Wing-back Chair
Barrel Chair
Charles of London

Before buying, please consider the size of the man in the house who will be using the furniture. Too often a small woman ruins the charm of her home with undersized furnishings, and the man in her life is never comfortable. Also, check seat heights. Very few guests like to flop down into enormous, overstuffed chairs. Many have back problems and may sue for injuries!

The Environmental Climate

Variableness of weather, rapid changes in temperature, heat, cold, humidity, and dryness all create the *environmental climate* for our possessions and dictate our approach to daily care, preservation of prized possessions, and prevention of problems.

All furniture and furnishings are classified as either *organic* or *inorganic* materials. Wood, textiles, leather, paper, fur, feathers, bone, ivory, parchment, basketry, etc. are organic—animal or vegetable matter. Metals and their alloys—gold, silver, copper, pewter, tin, iron, steel—and ceramics, glass, bricks, etc., are inorganic materials.

All organic materials are shocked by sudden or alternating changes of temperature, dryness, and moisture. Inorganic objects do not require as much protection as items of organic origin.

The condition of any object changes when it becomes worn, rots, corrodes, or breaks, and it should be stressed that these changes are directly due to environmental climate, improper storage, or careless handling.

All these factors can be controlled, but breakage and incorrect handling, particularly in the home, probably accounts for most problems. Museums insist that any object being moved must be held with two hands. Oil or sweat mingling with dust on an object can be damaging and may not show for weeks after the surface has been touched.

When shipping, moving, or storing becomes necessary, engage a professional packer to help you or allow the packer to do the entire job.

RELATIVE HUMIDITY

To pamper our possessions and create a stable environmental climate for them in the home, the moisture or humidity in all areas must be adjusted to room temperature winter and summer. Adjusting the humidity, or moisture, percentage to room temperature is called relative humidity (r.h.). For example, if the thermostat is set for 68 to 70 degrees Fahrenheit, the relative humidity should register 40 to 60 percent. Low humidity, insufficient moisture in hot or overheated rooms, or high humidity in cold rooms is equally destructive to our possessions.

HYGROMETERS

Every house or office should be equipped with one or more hygrometers (humidity gauges) to show the humidity percentage of your environment. Hygrometers can be bought at most hardware stores. Silver hygrometers can be purchased at jewelry stores, and are most efficient. Some are made with combination humidity gauge and thermometer. This item is small enough to sit on a desk or table and makes an unusual and practical gift.

EXCESSIVE MOISTURE

High humidity without ventilation is a particularly destructive force. Furniture, textiles, even metals, can be ruined if stored over-long in damp, sunless, airless rooms, attics, or cellars. Wood warps, veneer lifts, inlay loosens, drawers swell and stick, and fabrics mold, fade, and disintegrate, metals corrode.

AIR-CONDITIONING

Air-conditioning is the answer to high humidity problems. Whether central air-conditioning or individual units are used, humidity can be controlled; filtered air is kept in circulation, and room-temperature may be thermostatically set to maintain any desired degree Fahrenheit. The "comfort zone" for humans ranges from 68° to 72° but certain art treasures may demand a cooler atmosphere so consult with museum experts for advice on environmental needs.

The tempered air flow created by air-conditioning systems means the air is being dehumidified but if the cooling capacity is underestimated for a house or a room and the dehumidifying is inadequate, people experience an unpleasant, chilly, clammy sensation. Seek the advice of engineers specializing in air-conditioning to install your system or to correct your problem.

HUMIDITY PROBLEMS

Mildew

Mildew (mold), a microscopic parasitic fungi, is common in climates of continuous high humidity or where there are periods of excessive moisture.

Mildew appears as a grey or white fuzzy mold and can be found on anything—clothing, furniture, textiles, leather, paintings, wallpaper, china, etc., and if not detected will eat through paper fibers to destroy books or manuscripts.

To successfully combat mildew, install a central air-conditioning system or individual units in rooms to control the humidity percentage. Good air circulation in all areas is imperative.

If you find mildew, the following tips may help:

Move any mildewed item into the air and sunshine to dry the material, or place an electric fan in the area to create good airflow.

All textiles, clothes, draperies, mattresses, pillows should be dried and then brushed to remove the mold. Better still, have important items dry-cleaned by a professional.

Mildew will attach to glass or china stored in damp, airless rooms or cabinets. To remove the mold, wash each item with warm, soapy water to which ammonia or vinegar has been added. Rinse well and dry thoroughly before returning to storage.

Watch your books; mold is very destructive to paper. It causes brown spots or "foxing."

Mildew on painted woodwork should be removed by a professional painter. Mildew on wallpaper is almost impossible to remove without smearing the surface texture and fading the colors. If the paper is valuable, I urge you to discuss cleaning methods with a museum curator, interior decorator, or a skilled painter. The paper may be ruined in the hands of an amateur.

To minimize mildew in closets or small storage areas, a variety of electric devices are available commercially. Be sure to allow some kind of airflow in these areas. A small metal screen inserted in or above the closet door is efficient and not noticeable if painted the color of the door.

Termites

Termites (flying ants) feast on wooden house foundations that are damp and eat their way up the inside wood structure. Termites can be a serious problem in new houses as well as old ones, so if ants with white wings are seen flying about or crawling along the floor, call an exterminator company and have a complete inspection made of your house and nearby trees to determine their hideaway. Delay can be disastrous and expensive.

Dry rot

Old wood is subject to a fungus disease known as dry-rot which develops rapidly in moist, airless areas. Flooring, timbers, wood paneling in houses that have been closed for months or years are often found infected with these fungus spores. Unfortunately, when the tell-tale powder heaps of dust are discovered, the disease is often beyond control and the fine old wood is ruined.

Treatment of dry-rot needs the knowledge and techniques of a specialist in wood.

These brief warnings emphasize the importance of moisture control in the *environmental climate* of furniture and furnishings. Humidity control can be achieved in this age of technical know-how and engineering by correcting air-circulation, by dehumidifying, and by stabilizing the temperature to suit the needs of furnishings or art objects.

EXCESSIVE DRYNESS

The natural dry air of arid climates preserves some materials (rather than destroys, as does excess moisture) but conditions of dryness in the environmental climate and lack of oxygen and moisture, created by over-heating, can cause serious problems.

For example, when wood becomes extremely dry it cracks or buckles; if the piece is veneered, the veneer lifts and any small inlaid bits fall out of the design. Fabrics and animal skins disintegrate. Any one of these problems makes repair difficult, expensive, and sometimes impossible.

HUMIDIFIERS

Dry, over-heated areas are as bad for people as they are for furnishings, so correct such problems by installing *humidifiers* in each room or by a central, *humidifying system*. The initial expense is small when compared with the cost of repairing or replacing your possessions and your doctor's bills!

ATMOSPHERIC POLLUTION

The seepage of industrial air-pollution and smog into our homes is almost impossible to combat. Air conditioning the home is the only control now available.

Dust has always been a problem in the home or office; in fact, it is constantly around us, settling onto and into all our possessions. Dust is a destructive force because the sharp edge of dust particles cuts textiles and paper, etches glass, and scratches fine furniture surfaces. Until the advent of air conditioning and electrostatic dust-collectors, it has been a particularly destructive force in museums and for private collections of art.

Those who live in arid areas of the country, where sandstorms are all too frequent, know that the only remedy to control deterioration of our possessions is to keep doors and windows shut tight, vacuum and dust often, and wherever possible, install a central air-conditioning system with good humidification.

At the seashore, the atmosphere mixed with salt crystals and moist sand is called "sea dust." This pollution, carried by blowing winds and fog, attacks all organic materials and objects.

If *sea dust* is allowed to remain any length of time on inorganic items, such as silver, copper, brass, bronze, pewter, even chrome, deterioration can be rapid, and in a short time your treasure is ruined. Sea dust is also destructive to all ceramics and glass.

Warning: Keep all such items washed, dry, and free from sea dust at all times—if possible.

Moist sea dust knows no limits. It can ruin leather, fur, framed prints, manuscripts, even oil paintings. Be sure to watch your books. Moist sea sand will infiltrate bookcases that are apparently tightly closed. Pages develop brown spots or "foxing," leather or linen bindings crack, come unglued, and the book falls apart; the result is a valuable book almost beyond repair.

Fabrics fade, become limp from the moist air, and will in time disintegrate. *My best advice* is to use washable curtains and bedspreads. Slipcover rather than upholster your furniture—cotton or linen will be the easiest materials to handle. Synthetic textiles could be a problem in this climate.

I know what it is to live near the sea. For many years I spent the summer months on Cape Cod. Though air conditioning the house could have kept our furnishings safe, who would want to close the windows to the breeze and roar of the sea!

Window glass and *exterior paint* can be completely ruined by sea dust during a windstorm because the sand etches the glass, and the salt crystals in the moist air then seal the sand onto window panes. *Wash down the windows* with a strong spray of water from a hose. Wash the doors and as much exterior paint as possible.

Caution: Don't forget your automobile. Wash the windshield and windows often, or you won't be able to see through the glass to drive. Sea dust can ruin the paint too!

PARTY AIR-POLLUTION

Oxygen is as vital to inanimate objects as it is to plant-life and humans. The atmosphere in airless, smoke-filled, over-heated rooms is just as bad for fabrics, silver, rugs, etc., as it is for you.

When a party is an hour or two old, the air—if you can call it that—is not much more than fall-out from cigarette smoke and carbon dioxide laden with little germs that spread colds and coughs. If headaches are the result of such conditions for humans, think of what has happened to the furnishings subjected to this smog!

The cigarette smoke that clings to draperies and impregnates overstuffed chairs, sofas, pillows, and rugs is difficult to eradicate. These dust particles, suspended in party-smog, contribute to fiber decay and silver tarnish. To emphasize this statement, I was told recently that non-marijuana smokers may always detect the sweet odor of "pot" the moment they enter a room—so remember, draperies and rugs have no secrets.

To prevent air stagnation, before the guests arrive:

Open a window and leave it open. Some guests will complain, but don't give in; insist oxygen adds to party pleasure.

Turn down the thermostat to at least $68°$—$65°$ is better still—because body warmth will soon heat the room.

After the guests leave, open several windows to air out the rooms, or turn on the air-conditioning unit. The oxygen will clear the polluted air, and your lungs.

ELECTROSTATIC AIR-CLEANER

One of the greatest boons to the health of the family and the furnishings is the electrostatic dust collector. These units are available as console or table models or they may be attached to hot-air recirculating heating systems. The electrostatic air-cleaner is the answer for asthmatic patients, children's playrooms, or for areas where art treasures are kept. Under such conditions, fabrics flourish and rugs last longer. Dusting is reduced to almost nil in winter when doors and windows are closed. Even when windows are open in summer, the machine does a good job.

Wood

In this modern age of urban living we tend to forget, or perhaps have never realized, the beauty and importance of our great forests. Since the beginning of time, wood has responded to the needs of men and has often been his practical or artistic inspiration.

Wood, the chief product of the forest, has built our houses, and warmed our hearths, cooked our food and supplied our homes with furniture. It was wood that first spanned our rivers and gave us boats to sail the seas; without wood, America might not have been discovered. Wooden ties have carried the burden of steel rails and trains to bind together cities, towns, and countries, The first wheel was only a thick slice of a tree trunk.

Some of the earliest eating utensils used by primitive man were made of wood and we are told it was the American Indian who taught our ancestors to make wooden "hollow-ware." Old Indian recipes have been found that tell of the medicinal properties of trees; swamp-laurel was used for diarrhea; slippery elm cured sore throat; black elder ointment soothed skin infections; and ground aspen-bark was used as a substitute for quinine.

The word *wood* we use so commonly comes from the Anglo-Saxon *widu*, meaning tree. The properties of wood include durability, strength, hardiness, workability, beauty of grain, and texture. Wood is further defined as hardwood or softwood. *Hardwood* usually means broadleaf or deciduous trees. *Softwood* indicates conifers or evergreens. But this identification can be very confusing because some conifers are deciduous and lose their leaves.

Bark, the protective covering of trees, helps to identify a species and is an important natural product that is used by many industries for many purposes.

Colonists built their houses of soft wood—pine, spruce and cedar— but cabinetmakers, who had migrated from the old country, knew from experience that the hardwood of chestnut, elm, oak and walnut, made the finest furniture. It was not until years later that mahogany imported from Cuba, Africa and South America was available for making furniture.

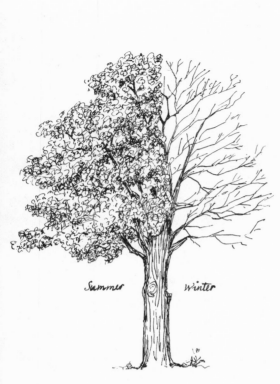

Deciduous Hardwood   *Evergreen Softwood*

VENEER

Veneering is hardly a new art. It is now known that cross-bonded veneers of wood were used to build Egyptian war boats around 2000 B.C. and the beautiful Thuya wood was imported by Egyptians to veneer their finest furniture. During the first century A.D., Pliny complained in his Natural History, that Roman merchants were selling ebony-veneered native cedar furniture as solid ebony—and were getting a higher price than for pieces made of genuine ebony.

Veneering or cross-bonding means alternating the grain-direction of succeeding layers of wood from *face* veneer through to *back* veneer which sets up counteracting forces within the *bonded* sheet. As a result, warpage of wood in one direction is cancelled out by warpage at right angles in the next sheet, and the whole panel remains stable. Veneer-bonded construction, for both the flat and curved parts of most furniture, is superior in at least three important ways.

1. It is more stable than solid wood.

2. It offers a wider range of grain designs, grain matches, and unusual figures on furniture.

3. It delivers the most exotic and expensive hardwoods at relatively modest cost.

CARE OF VENEERED FURNITURE

Veneers are affected by heat, dryness, and excessive moisture. All veneered furniture should therefore be kept in the proper environmental climate, cleaned regularly, and waxed as needed.

In the wrong environment the veneer can lift or blister, and these problems are not easy to cure if dust or dirt has seeped beneath. Only a restorer of fine furniture can repair such problems.

MARQUETRY

Marquetry, or inlay, is a decorative process in which elaborate patterns are formed by cutting and then inserting small pieces of colorful woods, fruit-woods, shells, ivory, even metals, gold, silver, or brass, into a wood veneer that is then applied and glued to the wood surface of a piece of furniture.

Marquetry has been created by great craftsmen. Treasure any piece, and give it special care! Of utmost importance is the relative humidity of the room.

Keep marquetry pieces away from direct sunlight, heat, and air-conditioning vents.

Dust carefully, being sure not to lift or loosen bits of valuable inlay.

At least twice a year gently apply a *thin coat* of *fine wax* to protect the surface from moisture, cracking, and stains. To wax marquetry, I use Antiquax or Goddard's.

PATINA

Regardless of the period or style, furniture is made of either *close-grained* hardwood or *open-grained* softwood, and the difference in wood texture usually dictates the finish used by craftsmen-of-old or modern manufacturers. It is important therefore, to determine the type of wood your furniture is made of and its *original finish*, before using any kind of polishing or cleaning agent.

The *patina* or original finish on antique wood *surfaces* is evidence of age and loving care. To the experienced eye, this patina often reflects the period or country in which a piece was made because cabinet-makers, through the years, have used different techniques and materials to finish wood surfaces. Sun bleach on the surface of an old or antique table also indicates age and adds a pleasant quality and beauty. Ink stains or blemishes on an old desk add romance, and pique our imagination about its original owner.

Any piece is far more valuable if the patina has not been disturbed. The value of many an antique has been reduced thousands of dollars because an amateur scraped off the original patina and attempted to put a glossy new finish on a fine old piece.

WOOD DESERVES SPECIAL CARE

It is of utmost importance that furniture be kept at all times in an environment of proper temperature, humidity and dryness because wood is organic. It swells under moist, humid conditions and contracts when it dries.

Gradual changes of temperature do not affect wood, but if the environmental climate suddenly moves from extreme cold to extreme heat, furniture is immediately subjected to stress. So if during a vacation your house has been kept cold or at a low temperature, don't immediately push the thermostat to 68° or above, on your return home—all the furnishings will suffer, not the furniture alone. Valuable furniture must be kept as far away as possible from radiators and cold-air vents.

WAXING UNSEEN PLACES

Any piece of furniture worth having should be protected by waxing both *inside* and *out*. Wood pieces, whether old or new, need wax on unseen areas, such as backs of cabinets; undersides of tables, chairs, and chests; insides of drawers and drawer-runners.

To protect these unseen areas melt any good paste wax slowly, over low heat. While the wax is still warm and soft enough to spread easily, using a painters one-inch brush, cover all surfaces carefully and apply enough wax to seep into the wood grain. Repeat every six months. Polishing hidden areas is not necessary.

CARE OF CLOSE-GRAINED HARDWOOD

These wood surfaces are usually sealed with varnish, lacquer or shellac, and require wax for protection and polishing—*not oil*. Wood that is waxed and well polished is protected from moisture or dryness and minor scratches, but wax alone does not create the patina—wax is only the means to an end, it is the *friction* and *heat*, created by repeated polishings, that gives the mirror-like finish. Cabinetmakers and restorers still believe the old adage that "bees-wax and elbow-grease" are the best polishing agents for furniture.

Bees-wax in its purest form is difficult to obtain, but fortunately several fine bees-wax products, formulated with other ingredients in either paste or liquid form, are made by American and English companies and may be purchased from antique dealers, furniture restorers, or up-to-date kitchenware departments.

I prefer *paste wax* because it gives protection and with frequent polishing, encourages a fine patina. Even paste wax, used for polishing floors is excellent, if thinly applied and "elbow-grease" used often.

For waxing or polishing wood surfaces I save old percale sheets, cut or tear the cloth into 30- or 36-inch squares, then fold into a thick pad of about 6 to 8 inches wide; this comfortably fits the palm of the hand for pushing back and forth across the table surface. I was taught this easy polishing method by "Frenchy," a world famous cabinetmaker in New Orleans, but he said "polish with the grain of the wood, and allow the wax to harden or set an hour or more before buffing."

Caution: avoid liquid, commercial products that promise to clean, wax, and polish your furniture, all in one application. Their claims may be valid but to liquify the wax, certain chemicals must be added. After several applications, the chemicals begin to fight the lacquer, varnish, or shellac finish, the wood surface becomes tacky or sticky, and the piece is ruined. When this happens, the surface must be stripped and the original finish is destroyed.

I have a friend who used one of these liquid-wax products on her husband's desk. That evening when he finished reading a valuable leather-bound book, he placed it on the desk; the next morning he found that his beautiful book had adhered to the wood—the book was ruined!

EXCESS WAX

The question often arises whether wax that has built up on wood surfaces by repeated waxing should be removed before *rewaxing* furniture, wood panelling, or wood flooring. There are two simple answers to this question.

1. If the waxed surface has been kept dusted and polished it may not be necessary to remove the old wax. Try hand rubbing; the friction and heat generated may loosen any excess wax and restore the polish.

If this doesn't work, the wax can be softened by using a few drops of turpentine on a cloth—rub hard, remove excess wax, allow to dry, then buff.

2. When old wax plus dust has built up through the years, it will take infinite patience to remove the wax without disturbing the surface finish or patina. Please allow an expert restorer to handle such a condition.

Caution: carbon-tetrachloride is an excellent chemical to use for removing old wax but the fumes, if inhaled, can cause serious problems. Amateurs should not use this chemical product.

SUNLIGHT BLEACHES WOOD

Never place fine furniture where it can be baked by sunrays that penetrate window glass. It doesn't take long to bleach wood and the extreme heat dries the natural oils. Instead, place the piece where filtered sun-light will show the beauty of the wood's grain and the proportion of the object.

To prevent bleaching, here are a few hints:

Items such as matching chests, commodes, or consoles, when used in pairs in the same room should have their position in the room rotated every few months so that the wood-color will remain equal.

Dining-room tables should be turned every few months to maintain even color. "Stretchers," or panels used to elongate the dining table, should be taken out of the storage area several times a year and either placed in the table for a few days, or placed in an area where sunlight will help to maintain the dining-table color.

Open folding tables occasionally to expose the inside leaf to light for a few days.

PROTECT TABLETOPS WITH LACQUER

To comply with today's social needs, wood surfaces can now be protected from the moisture of cocktail glasses, alcohol, and flower vases by a method of lacquering that is safe to use, even on fine antique tables. But the lacquer has to be applied layer after layer under dry, warm conditions and *is no job for an amateur*. Have an expert restorer lacquer your tables. Such surfaces should be waxed and buffed.

Let me warn you, there is a new clear plastic product being advertised for lacquering, which sprays onto any wood surface, that promises not to chip, mar, peel, or flake, and to last twice as long as varnish. It can damage the patina of wood surfaces whether old or new. *Don't use* it, unless you are ruthless in your attitude towards wood.

WATER MARKS

A waxed surface cannot provide complete protection against damage if liquids or moisture from iced cocktail glasses are allowed to sit on a wood finish indefinitely. However, a well-waxed and polished surface will prevent moisture from being immediately absorbed, thus allowing time to wipe up the liquid.

WHITE STAINS ON WOOD SURFACES

White Stains on wood surfaces, caused by moisture from cocktail glasses or flower vases can be easily removed.

1. Mix cigarette or cigar ash with a little soft paste wax.
2. Apply to the area, rub gently.
3. Wipe clean and buff with a soft cloth.
4. Rewax the entire surface only if needed to blend the wax.

MILK OR DAIRY PRODUCT STAINS

If milk or foods containing milk or cream, such as ice cream or custard, are allowed to remain on wood surfaces, the lactic acid in the milk acts like a mild paint or varnish remover; therefore, wipe up spills as quickly as possible. If spots appear, apply wax, allow to harden, then polish. Any further repair should be done by a professional.

MINOR SCRATCHES OR BLEMISHES

For small scratches try using colored crayons, or wax sticks, that are especially made in furniture wood tones. These crayons are softer than an rdinary crayon and are easier to work with. Fill the scratch with crayon, ubbing well with your finger, then wipe with a soft dry cloth and polish. 'or more extensive damage, such as burns and blemishes that penetrate the arnish surface, consult a professional.

MAJOR SURFACES BLEMISHES

Cigarette burns that have penetrated the surface-finish should be re-aired by professionals.

Alcoholic beverages, perfumes, and *medicines* all cause irreparable damage o furniture surfaces because alcohol tends to dissolve varnish or lacquer. Vipe spills as quickly as possible. Wax then polish by rubbing vigorously.

TO REMOVE CANDLE WAX

To remove candle wax from dining-room tables or other wood sur-aces, soak a soft cloth in very hot water, wring dry, rub the wood surface, epeat until the wax is gone, wipe dry. Do not wax surface until completely ry. Usually the surface will only need polishing by rubbing with a cloth.

CARE OF OPEN-GRAINED SOFT WOOD

To oil or not to oil open-grained soft-wood surfaces is a highly con-roversial topic even among authorities, so I offer here what seems to ne the concensus of opinion on the subject plus my own experience. 3eyond that you are on your own.

For hundreds of years various oils have been used on open-grained, 1on-varnished wood surfaces to "feed" and polish the wood. According o some scientists, oil *does not feed* wood, it merely forms a coating that :hanges the refraction of light and makes the wood handsomer. But il darkens and changes the color of open-grained wood. Some museum uthorities, currently researching the care of wood, find that after repeated applications, oil enters the grain and congeals, thereby harden-ing wood texture. Furthermore, oil dries or evaporates and what remains on the surface only catches dust.

Actually, oil does *not* give a polished finish—it is the friction and heat created by rubbing that produces the beautiful patina. Instead of oil, use warm melted wax; it is an excellent substitute on open-grained wood surfaces.

Advice:

Furniture oil products—even lemon oil—removes surface dust

quickly but no matter how carefully the excess oil is removed, th
residue immediately begins collecting dust and grime! And remember–
do not use oil or oil products on varnished or any hard-finished woo
surfaces.

If you insist on using the oil method of so-called "feeding" oper
grained wood, here is an old formula to use:

1.   Mix— ⅓ boiled linseed oil
          ⅓ turpentine
          ⅓ white vinegar and a few drops of methylated spirits.
2. Apply sparsely to unsealed wood surface.
3. Wipe away all excess oil.
4. Polish with a clean, dry flannel cloth, rubbing with the grair
5. Repeat only when *absolutely* necessary.

Another formula that I'm told hardens and builds patina i
          ⅔ linseed oil
          ⅓ pure turpentine

Spread evenly over the surface, allow to dry fifteen minutes, the
polish with a flannel cloth.

WOODWORMS

Furniture or wood of any kind that is *old* and *dry* is especiall
susceptible to woodworms. Woodworms also attack sap-wood backin
on restored pieces. Hatched from various types of wood-boring beetle
the grubs tunnel into the wood and live in the holes as long as two year
Only when dust-like heaps of powder are found are we warned tha
grubs are at work. Any infected piece should be immediately placed ou
of doors and fumigated as a precaution against the spread of the problem

If, after fumigation, the piece shows further worm activity or if th
condition cannot be cured, the article must be burned. Old floor boarc
and timbers should be checked regularly for woodworms.

DRAWER PROBLEMS

Through years of use drawers and their runners become worn an
produce a fine dust. This condition is sometimes blamed on termites o
wood-worms, but it is most likely the rubbing of the drawer on it
runners that creates the powder-like dust, not wood-boring insect

If there are no visible worm-holes in the wood, soap or candl
wax rubbed on the drawer and runner will cure the problem.

Hot, humid weather causes drawer problems too; the wood swells—do nothing—when the weather changes the wood will shrink and the drawer return to normal size.

PAINTED WOODWORK OR FURNITURE

Furniture and woodwork that has been "antiqued" or glazed needs to be handled with care. Soap and water washing can remove the beautiful glaze.

Vacuum all woodwork regularly to prevent dust and polluted particles in the air from accumulating on the surface. Unglazed painted wood can be washed with mild soapsuds and water, carefully rinsed, and dried. Clean small areas at a time. Commercial cleansers formulated to care for painted woodwork are superior to soap and water.

MUSICAL INSTRUMENTS

Musical instruments made of wood need very special care. Moisture or high humidity and alternating periods of dryness and heat are destructive factors. Necks of violins, guitars, ukeleles, and similar instruments warp; the sounding board of a piano may crack. Many of these problems can only be corrected at tremendous expense, and often the instrument is permanently damaged.

Constant care of instruments is imperative:

1. Pianos and all stringed instruments must be kept in tune.

2. Prevent expansion or contraction of the wood by regularly applying a fine, specially designed wax product for such instruments.

3. Teach young people to protect and care for these valuable instruments.

PIANOS

Pianos are complex instruments built of many diverse and costly raw materials. There are more than 9,000 parts in the key and action combination alone. The piano is made of top-quality wood of many species: iron, steel, copper, brass, plastics, wool, cotton, various adhesives. Piano strings represent the highest development in steel wire; only a few steel companies manufacture piano wire.

There are more than 200 strings in a standard piano, and the combined tension of these strings exerts a pull of better than eighteen tons. These strings bear upon the sounding board by means of wooden bridges and a system of reverse bearings that practically lock the strings and wood together. It is important that each of these strings be kept at the proper tension or it will be off pitch—in other words, OUT OF TUNE!

Care of pianos

My best advice is to entrust your fine instrument to a qualified piano-tuner technician. Frequency of tuning depends on the amount of use the piano receives and its environmental climate. Moisture or high humidity and alternating periods of dryness and heat are destructive factors.

Piano cases are made of the finest wood available, not only for beauty but also for resonance and tonal quality. It is, therefore, important that your piano case be regularly waxed and rubbed with a good quality wax, such as you would use on fine furniture. Twice a year is usually enough to apply wax for protection from expansion and contraction. DO NOT use any commercial liquid wax, oil, or wax sprays, you may ruin the strings, sounding board, and felts.

1. Vacuum your piano regularly.

2. Beware of the larvae of clothes-moths that attack and feed on the felts.

3. The keyboard of the piano should remain open at all times for good air circulation.

4. Ivory keys turn yellow from age. Do not wash ivory keys with soap or ammonia. Wipe with a soft cloth that has been dipped in clear cold water. Dry thoroughly.

5. Other types of keys can be cleaned the same way.

WOOD FLOORS

Stone or tiles covered the floors in the earliest homes of Europe. These floors were cold and rugs non-existent until strips of matting, made of plaited reeds were devised. Floors in old France in those days, were covered with straw or rushes, then strewn with scented herbs.

Centuries later rare hardwood began to be used for flooring in palaces and manor houses. Those who could not afford hardwood floors, hoarded prized bits of these costly woods, then matched, sawed, and fitted them into intricate patterns and unknowingly created parquetry flooring.

HARDWOOD OR PARQUETRY FLOORS

This type of flooring is usually stained to a chosen color, sanded, then varnished. Hard-finished floors require *paste floor wax* to protect the surface from scuff marks and scratches, and to develop and maintain a mirror-like patina.

Never use commercial liquid or spray waxes, particularly the ones that guarantee to clean and polish in one application. Some of these products create a sticky surface that collects dust and dirt.

1. Vacuum hardwood floors regularly to remove dirt and grit.
2. Wax, by applying a thin coat of any well-known paste-floor-wax.
3. Allow wax to dry an hour, then buff to a high polish.

Caution: Do not wash hardwood floors with soap and water. If surface stains must be removed, use a *moist*—not wet—cloth or mop.

Old wax and dirt that has built up on neglected floors has to be removed to rejuvenate the finish. This is a tedious job; whenever possible have a professional do the work.

1. Old wax can be loosened by applying turpentine or a good commercial wax remover.
2. Mop up the loosened wax.
3. After 24 hours the surface should be dry, re-wax and polish the floor.

The electric floor waxer-polisher

This appliance has brushes for waxing, polishing, even for scrubbing and removing old wax. Every home should have one. If that's not possible, they can be rented.

POLYURETHANE SYNTHETIC SURFACE FINISH

Polyurethane is a liquid synthetic plastic varnish that is available in high gloss or satin finish for finishing wood flooring. This synthetic varnish scuffs easily, shows dust and dirt, and in time may "crackle." If this surface cracks, the only remedy is to scrape, sand, and refinish the entire floor! That's expensive.

WIDE-BOARD FLOORING

Wide boards cut from pine, maple, cherry or walnut covered the floors of the homes of the earliest American colonists but by law, boards were not allowed to be cut more than 24 inches wide. This order of the Crown meant that trees larger than 24 inches or "King-size" trees were reserved for the King's Royal Navy for building ships. Severe punishment resulted from the cutting of these trees.

Colonists must have complied with the law for very few old homes or buildings have been found floored with boards wider than two feet. Contrary to popular belief these early floorboards were not secured with wooden screws or pegs. The surface nails used were made of bog or "pig-iron" and the blacksmith came to the job to make the necessary nails.

Care of wide-board flooring

The wood used for wide-board flooring was left open-grained, then oiled to darken the color and to protect the wood. Such flooring is extremely valuable and should be treated with loving care. However, instead of using oil, try melted floor paste-wax, it will give better protection, collect less dust and develop a beautiful patina. Be sure to vacuum the floor often.

Caution: Wide-board wooden floors must not be washed with soap and water. The moisture that seeps between and underneath the boards invites wood-rot and termites, and mars the beautiful color of the wood.

Lacquer

LACQUERWARE originated in China at the dawn of her history and ranks with silk, pottery, porcelain, paper, and printing among China's contributions to world culture.

Lacquer is one of the most durable of all natural substances. Lacquerware excavated from flooded tombs appears as new and bright as when it was made, after being immersed for 2000 years.

Oriental lacquer is made from the sap of the Chinese Tsi or Lac tree, a deadly poisonous Sumac that grows wild in all parts of China, particularly at very high altitudes. The lac tree is also indigenous to Korea. It is believed that centuries past, China taught the Japanese the art of lacquering and introduced to Japan cuttings and seeds of the *Rhus Vernicifera* that led to the development of their great Lac plantations.

The technique of extracting lac has not changed with time. When a tree is eight to ten years old, the bark is slashed horizontally and the lac collected in copper cups, in much the same way as rubber. As the resin oozes out, it appears as a transparent, whitish sap which immediately thickens and darkens on contact with air, and hardens so quickly it cannot be readily dissolved. To be used, lac must be submitted to prolonged boiling, skimming, then filtering through hemp cloth to remove earth and vegetable impurities.

The quality of ancient Chinese and Japanese lacquer-work has never been equalled. Coat after coat of lac was delicately and slowly applied, and each coat allowed to dry in a damp, dark, and dust-free chamber, otherwise the lacquer could become fragile and flake off. When the lacquer hardened, the surface was buffed to a satin-smooth finish before the next coat was brushed on. If the lacquered surface was to be flat or incised, thirty or more coats were applied. If the surface was to be carved, a hundred to three hundred coats would be needed. After a craftsman had completed the lacquering, an artist added the decoration to complete the work of art.

Craftsmen in ancient China prized lacquer for its inherent resistance to dampness, rot, and woodworms. Lacquer was applied to silk hats, leather shoes, wooden furniture, and coffins. Armorers, saddlers and wheelwrights used it as protective covering on sword hilts, scabbards, stirrups and spokes of wheels.

Lacquering was the product of artisans of infinite patience, remarkable skill, sureness of touch, and fine artistic sense. These lacquer workers appear to have been greatly esteemed because during the Han Dynasty in China, credit was given to each artist or craftsman participating in the manufacture of a piece. One small Han vessel is marked with the name of the painter and lacquerer, gilder, engraver, director, sub-director, assistant, sub-assistant, and official.

Lacquer is considered a protective cover for wood; however, if the lacquer is fractured; the wood underneath is at once subject to moisture or dryness. If cracks occur in Oriental lacquer, it is almost impossible to restore because of its extreme hardness and insolubility, more so in proportion to the number of coats that were previously applied.

The finest lacquered pieces of the 17th and 18th centuries were imported to Europe from China, Japan or Korea. European craftsmen imitated but were never capable of creating the beauty of Oriental lacquerware, primarily because European lacquer was a mixture of varnish, paint, and shellac and not made of the gum of a true Lac tree. These craftsmen did develop a method of lacquering that became known as Japaning.

Dust lacquerware with an artist's brush. Accumulated dust or soot may be washed off with mild soap and warm water. Rinse and dry carefully.

The lacquer on very old furniture if dry and brittle is easily chipped. Be cautious when vacuuming the floor. If the appliance hits the lacquer, any pieces that chip off will be difficult to replace. Relacquering would be almost impossible.

SHELLAC

Shellac, another resinous substance, is secreted by a scale insect that lives on various trees and is extensively cultivated in India.

Commercial shellac made of this gum is white or orange in color, has excellent sealing qualities and dries quickly, but like all lacquer it must be applied under damp, warm conditions. If this fundamental is ignored, the finished coat may develop a cloudy appearance known as "blooming."

Textiles

WHEN man invented the art of weaving, textiles became the main factor in the economic history of many great civilizations, so it is to textiles that we turn for clues to man's early ways of life.

The *four natural* fibers from which cloth was woven are wool, silk, linen, and cotton. Each fiber traces its origin back into the centuries and has woven its own story, wool to prehistoric times, silk to China, linen to Egypt, and cotton to India.

History records that in 4000 B.C., Egyptians knew how to fabricate cloth and the art of preparing dyes, which still defy the corrosion of time.

Millenniums later, the textile trade became so important in Europe that France, in the 13th century, found it necessary to supervise the industry by creating the Weavers Guild. Laws were passed that gave the Guild powers that controlled the trade for 700 years or until the advent of power looms.

When the destructive religious wars ended in France, late in the 16th Century, cloth was scarce—so scarce that Henry IV claimed he was the "poorest sovereign ever to be crowned; that he had only twelve shirts and most of them had holes." He also claimed twelve handkerchiefs, but was corrected by his valet with a terse, "Only eight, Sire!"

Perhaps because of his own personal needs, one of Henry IV's first projects, after ascending the throne of France, was to re-establish the textile industry.

The story of the great textile trade is told in scenes throughout France: in Orléans one walks along Great Scissors Street, Wool Combers Street, or The Street of the Hand That Weaves! At Amiens, the stained glass windows in the Cathedral were presented by the drapers and dyers who worked in Thread Square. In Reims, a sermon is cut into stone on the Cathedral that tells of the dishonest draper who "cut his cloth short!" One of France's greatest arts and industries was her glorious woven wool tapestries.

When weaving became economically important in many European countries, serge, a drab, heavy wool fabric, gave way to the new imports, and looms began to produce silks, brocades, velvets, and later, linens and cottons.

During the reigns of Louis XIV and Louis XV in France, the weaving of silk, linen, and cotton reached a zenith of beauty and perfection probably never surpassed. In the 19th century, England became preeminent in the development of weaving linen and cotton textiles.

BUYING TEXTILES

If you are a novice doing your first house or apartment, seek professional advice, for fabrics, textures, designs, and color combinations can enhance or ruin your decorating scheme, and any mistake is expensive.

Should the fabric you choose for color and texture be beyond the limits of your budget—keep searching. Less expensive substitutes *can* be found and often prove to be more pleasing in color and more serviceable in texture. Many glorious synthetic fabrics or synthetics combined with silk or cotton are available today, so the price per yard need not be a factor. Experience teaches us that by careful shopping, excellent, inexpensive substitutes are waiting in the fabulous fabric houses.

Whenever possible, ask a decorator or a friend who has a decorator's license to take you into fabric "show" rooms. Here you learn to evaluate color, color combinations, and fabric texture, and texture is of utmost importance in balancing any decorating scheme. In some of the larger fabric houses you can also become acquainted with carpeting and rugs. For the novice, this can be a fascinating experience and a liberal education in decorating. But, be sure to check the price tag on all fabrics and floor coverings!

DRY-CLEANING TEXTILES

The term "dry cleaning" is a misnomer because fabrics when "dry-cleaned" are subjected to chemical wetting.

Dry cleaning is a highly developed science. Before a fabric is cleaned, a test is made to determine the types of fibers in the material and what caused the stain. On the basis of this analysis the technician decides what chemicals to use. If the stain cannot be removed without harming the fabric, a responsible dry-cleaning company will refuse to clean the item.

My best advice is to always discuss cleaning problems with someone skilled in the newest dry-cleaning methods.

CARE OF DRAPERIES AND UPHOLSTERY

Protection of fabrics used for draperies and upholstery is important,

because these fabrics are rarely washable and some are quite difficult
to clean.

PREVENT FABRIC FADING

Protect draperies and upholstery from direct sunlight. Window glass
magnifies the destructive elements in the sun's rays and snow reflection
can be equally bad; air-pollution also causes fading.

To prevent these problems:

1. Draw the blinds to cut sun rays.

2. Use summer awnings.

3. Draperies last longer and are protected from fading if they are
lined—better still, lined and interlined.

If there are large areas of glass in your home, investigate the new
colorless, transparent product being sprayed onto glass in museums,
churches, office buildings, and private residences to deflect destructive
sun rays and eliminate fabric fading.

Drapes should be cleaned only when absolutely necessary because
regardless of the method used, they are often ruined beyond redemption.
In the cleaning process, the main or outside fabric may either shorten or
lengthen, and the interlining, or lining, goes its own separate way.

Vacuum the drapes regularly to avoid accumulation of dust.

Fabrics breathe and absorb moisture, so don't be surprised if your
curtains shrink lengthwise as much as three inches, and then, with the
change of weather, return to their normal length.

SPOT-CLEANING FABRICS

Spot-cleaning upholstery is difficult and can be disastrous: But, if
you have had an accident and must do the cleaning yourself:

1. Use a cleaning fluid recommended by a dry-cleaning company.
Work inward, to control the size of the stain.

2. To dry the cleaning fluid, lightly brush the spot with a towel.
Do not rub—rubbing may tear the fabric or the superficial threads on
fine brocades.

STORING FINE FABRICS

1. Fabrics need air—without it they disintegrate. Never store valuable fabrics in trunks or sealed boxes. Sealed or zippered plastic bags
may trap moisture and cause rot, fading, and disintegration of fibers.

2. Treasured fabrics should not be folded. If folding is necessary, refold at intervals, reversing the fold. Lengths of wadded tissue paper placed in the fold of the fabric add protection.

Use old sheets

If a home is to be closed for any length of time furniture and fabrics must be protected, for dust and air-pollution particles seep in no matter how tightly doors and windows are closed.

Plastic covers are available but the old-fashioned use of sheets, thrown over furnishings is still the safest protection. Your rooms may resemble a "Charles Addams" setting but the cloth will catch the dust, is washable, reusable and does not trap moisture, as does plastic.

WOOL

Wool is the fiber forming the protective covering of sheep. The outside of wool fiber is made up of flat, over-lapping, irregular scales which look like shingles on a roof! These fibers grow with a "crimp" or wavy form, giving excellent properties of elasticity and resilience and they vary in length from short to long, and are fine or coarse. Basically, the fineness and length of the fiber determines whether the fleece will be classified as "apparel class wool" or "carpet wool."

Hundreds of varieties of sheep are raised all over the world for different purposes: some for meat alone, some for their wool, and others for both meat and wool. Sheep's wool is removed once a year. To remove the wool, sheep-shearers use a power machine resembling barbers' clippers—an expert can shear 100 to 200 sheep a day! As the sheep is shorn, great sheets of fleece roll off! These bundles are tied, sorted, then sent to the mills where the wool is washed or cleaned before being processed.

Sheep, one of the first animals domesticated by man, has furnished his basic necessities, food and cloth, through the ages. Yet it is impossible to pin-point the time in history when sheep were first shorn and wool fibers spun into thread for weaving. Bits of wool fabric, unearthed in the ruins of Neolithic villages, record the use of wool in this period and other evidence indicates that by the year 3000 B.C., all Asiatic tribes were breeding and raising sheep to supply their people with food and clothing.

By the Middle Ages, wool weaving was a flourishing industry in

Venice and Florence. In A.D. 1340 Italy was employing 30,000 workers in the wool trade.

The finest wool comes from the Spanish strain of native Merino sheep. From A.D. 1400 for about 300 years, the Spanish improved their Merino strain and exportation through those years was punishable by death. Late in the 17th century, France began importing Merinos; in the next 100 years, Spanish Merinos were being raised in many countries.

To develop their wool industry, England in the 1400's adopted a policy of inviting wool craftsmen to settle in Britain. This successful plan made England the leading wool textile producers of that era.

Sheep were not native to America, but were brought to the new world by Coronado, the Spanish explorer. Wool growing was slow to develop in America, so colonists depended on England for wool supplies and woven wool cloth. Beginning in 1801, Americans began importing Merinos from Spain and France to improve domestic strains and by 1810, 24 woolen mills were operating in New England; thus began the history of the manufacture of carpeting and rug making in America.

Domesticated sheep are now raised in every country of the world, but the Merino is, once again, a jealously guarded strain that is bred chiefly in Australia.

In France during the reign of Louis XIII, *wool* was woven into serge and used for upholstery and draperies. When Louis XIV came to the throne, these dark and somber wool textiles were replaced in palaces and homes with the more luxurious silks, brocades, velvets, damasks, and brocatelles made of Oriental silk.

TAPESTRIES AND WALL HANGINGS

In Medieval times stones and plastered walls were hung with woven wool tapestries and sometimes, with elaborately embroidered hangings. Used primarily to cover cracks in the walls of feudal castles, these tapestries kept out cold and dampness, and added a touch of luxury.

Heavy woolen tapestries were replaced in the 18th century by carved panels of oak or walnut. In France, these elaborately carved panels called "boiseries" covered the walls of palaces and manor houses from floor to ceiling. When mirrors and tapestries began to be set into the panelling, tapestries took on a new dimension. Designed by the greatest artists of France and woven by master weavers on the looms of the fabulous textile factories, woven wool tapestries became pictures and competed in beauty with oil paintings.

Some of the most glorious wall hangings of all time were woven in Old China of silk, combinations of silk, wool and sometimes gold threads and even fine grasses. Of necessity these textiles must be handled with infinite care. If you own such a treasure discuss its care with the curator of a museum or an authority on Chinese textiles.

Take care of old tapestries and wall hangings:

Tapestries and wall hangings, whether wool or silk, must occasionally be removed from the wall, carefully rolled, and allowed to rest. The stress caused by continuous hanging produces a strain on the warp and, therefore, unnecessary deterioration.

These materials are organic. Excess moisture or dryness are destructive factors.

1. Keep all wall hangings away from strong light to prevent fading.

2. Creases or folds created by careless hanging will eventually cut threads and cause streaky fading. See to it that such hangings are hung smoothly.

3. If valuable tapestry becomes fragile, you will need advice from a professional in needlework or the curator of a museum.

4. Only experts should be allowed to clean or mothproof valuable tapestries.

CARPETS AND RUGS

The stone and hard-packed earth of man's earliest abode was covered with animal skins or with rushes. As his demands for comfort increased reeds began to be plaited into mats, following the ancient art of basketry. Fragments of such mats have been discovered in the Near East that date back to 6000 B.C. By medieval times the plaiting of reeds into mats had attained the status of an art in the Near East.

With the domestication of wool-bearing animals, about 7000 B.C., came the art of spinning wool fibers and weaving. Tufts of wool were saved, then tied with the reeds, close enough together to create a material that was pleasant to stand on, sit on, even to sleep under.

The word carpet derives from the Latin *carpere*, meaning to pluck or card, as wool. In old French the word *carpite* described a coarse cloth that was used for wrapping packages to be carried on the backs of men or animals. *Rug* is a Scandinavian word meaning rough, coarse cloth.

The art of carpet weaving progressed rapidly in the cold mountain areas of Persia, Turkey, Syria. People with time and patience combined wool, camel's hair or goat's hair on flaxen warp. These fabrics were woven by hand on the crudest looms and were almost indestructible under ordinary wear. Carpets still cover the palace floors in Persia that have been there since the end of the 16th century.

The Saracens invaded France in A.D. 733 and were defeated in a battle near the village of Aubusson by Charles Martel, father of Charlemagne. Many Saracen soldiers skilled in the art of weaving rugs—a craft learned from their Oriental ancestors—settled in Aubusson and began to weave rugs.

When Henri IV (1589–1610) ascended the throne of France, he took these weavers under his protection and immediately forbade the importation of rugs. Aubusson weavers now began to follow the techniques of the tapestry industry. The genius of France's greatest artist was expended on designs for these rugs and the weaving was done by the most skilled craftsmen.

Aubusson rugs are unique. Both sides are alike though the reverse side shows more threads. The selvedge is turned under and the rug is lined. There is no fringe as in Orientals. Rug texture is firm, flat and quite thin, therefore useful for upholstery as well as for floor coverings.

The process of weaving Savonnerie rugs was supposedly invented in 1604 by Pierre Du Pont. When his method of weaving was presented to Henri IV, Du Pont was immediately ensconced in the artisans galleries of the Louvre to weave rugs for the Court. The venture was so successful the industry was moved and housed in part of an old soap factory in Chaillot and became known as Savonnerie, meaning soap.

Part of the old soap factory was used as a home for orphaned children. This arrangement assured cheap labor as well as space. Twelve year old children were apprenticed in the factory and the Home paid a small fee for each child's work during the last eight years of apprenticeship. By the end of the term, the child was highly skilled and received a small portion of the accumulated money.

Savonnerie rugs are characterized by a deep, rich pile that gives the rugs a carved appearance. The oldest Savonnerie to be preserved was made for Cardinal Richelieu; the design is elaborate, the coloring dark, and is remarkable for the predominance of blacks. This rug may be seen in Paris.

Weaving done by the Navajo Indian in the United States is an excellent example of workmanship. Their rugs and blankets, laboriously woven by hand, are colored by native pigments and wear for many years.

The Spanish explorer, Hérnando Cortés, conquered Mexico in the 16th century and found the palaces of Montezuma covered with fabulous rugs. Many were made of animal skins. Others were made with the skins of humming-birds sewn together.

Some of the finest rugs are still being woven in Persia and India.

CARE OF FINE RUGS AND CARPETS

Dirt and grit that sifts into the base of the nap cuts and wears down the pile of rugs and carpets.

Shift the position of a rug every few months to prevent traffic-wear in one area and uneven fading.

Vacuum your rugs at least once a week working with, not against, the nap.

Fine rugs should be cleaned and moth-proofed once a year by a professional rug-cleaning establishment. Rugs to be stored any length of time are best cared for by professionals, for not only must they be moth-proofed, they must be rolled with the nap inside and tightly sealed. Only a rug or storage company can do this packing correctly.

All carpets and rugs must be vacuumed regularly, particularly under furniture and in dark areas to deter moths.

Many products are formulated for shampooing and dry-cleaning woolen rugs and carpets. Equipment can be rented to make the cleaning easier.

A word of warning:

Don't shampoo or chemically wet your rug or carpet the day of a party. If the humidity is high the pile will not dry within forty-eight hours, maybe longer.

When the dry-cleaning or shampooing has been completed place small squares of metal foil under the foot of every chair, table, etc. The foil is used to prevent rust stains that could result from metal gliders remaining on moist fabric.

Leave protectors in place until the pile is absolutely dry. The best protection is to replace all metal gliders with plastic gliders and thereby avoid problems.

SPOTS AND SPILLS

Remove spots or spills quickly. Coffee or tea spilled on wool will dye the pile. Soak up excess liquid with a sponge or cloth, then use clear cold water sparingly to remove as much of the stain as possible. Soap or detergents can set the stain.

PET STAINS CAN RUIN WOOL

As quickly as possible after the spot is discovered, soak the area with club soda. Blot with heavy absorbent cloth. Repeat process until spot disappears—dry thoroughly.

A formula of 1 oz. clear ammonia to 8 oz. of water may do the job. Rinse with clear cool water. Dry thoroughly to remove water deep in the pile.

If the stain has dried and turned brown, try any or all of the above suggestions.

MOTHS

These tiny winged insects breed in dark storage areas, in closets or under furniture and lay their eggs on any available wool, fabric, fur or feathers. Moths do not like silk, cotton, linen or synthetic fibers.

Within a week the worm-like larvae hatches and begins feeding on fur or feathers and chewing holes in woolen fabrics.

Sunlight, air and the vacuum cleaner are the moth's natural enemies.

Vacuum regularly, particularly in dark areas under furniture and in coat closets.

Fumes of paradi-chlorobenzine crystals deter moth-life if crystals are used in sufficient quantity.

The odor of cedar, pine, tar-paper and lavender will not deter the clothes-moth.

Moth-proofing aerosal sprays give excellent protection.

Dry-clean and moth-proof all woolens once a year.

Have all rugs, carpets, blankets, needlepoint or any woolen article dry-cleaned and moth-proofed before storing.

To store small rugs, dry-clean, cover the rug pile with paradi-chlorobenzine crystals, roll the rug with the pile inside, wrap with heavy paper and seal.

ORIENTAL RUGS ARE VALUABLE

Perhaps the most sumptuous Oriental floor covering ever devised was the carpet woven for King Khosrau II, a great monarch of the Sasanian dynasty and described in Arab documents. It lay on the floor of the vast audience chamber of the palace of Ctesiphon, and represented a formal garden, running brooks, paths, and flower beds of multiple colors worked in countless jewels. The earth and banks of the brooks were worked in gold; the running water was made of crystal-clear stones —probably diamonds. The gravel paths were paved with pearls; then the entire carpet was bordered with a solid band of emeralds, representing barley fields. The rug proclaimed the glory, wealth, and might of the great king and was a warning to enemies that it would be imprudent to challenge him.

This Oriental rug of overwhelming beauty was moreover a religious document demonstrating to all the glory of Paradise, the eternal and timeless garden, the ideal of happiness and of perfection. It exercised a never-ending influence on the art of Iran for rugs of this pattern have been woven ever since.

The carpet no longer exists. After the Islamic conquest the carpet was cut up and distributed as booty or sold in bits. It was estimated to be worth over $200,000,000.

Oriental rugs need special care

Old and valuable Oriental rugs that need cleaning must not be subjected to *chemical wetting*, the solvents used in the dry-cleaning process can cause the dyes to "run" or change color and remove the natural oil from the fibers.

These fine rugs should be *washed* by experts skilled in handling Orientals.

SILK

Silk fibers come from various moth caterpillars that spin a cocoon of silky threads. These moth caterpillars feed on the foliage of trees and shrubs and are particularly fond of the leaves of the white mulberry tree.

The silkworm is very temperamental. It is adversely affected by noise, vibrations, and strong odors and spins only top quality silk under the most propitious circumstances.

From the moment the insect emerges from its egg and begins its short, but busy life, it "spins" five days winding itself into 2,000—sometimes 3,000 feet—of two blended silk strands. These silk threads are produced by special glands, called *secteries*, that extend the entire length of the insect's body, terminating in *spinerets*, situated in the insect's mouth.

Within 15 to 20 days after the chrysalis has formed, the adult moth emerges, mates, lays its eggs on a convenient mulberry tree and dies—all in the same day! It is estimated that there are 20,000 to 40,000 eggs to an ounce and that one ounce of eggs yields 100 pounds of cocoons or 9 pounds of raw silk.

Silkworms are also endowed with a "silk sac" that is ready to use when the worm begins spinning its cocoon. If the cocoon is killed, the silky substance in the sac can be drawn into lustrous strong leaders called "gut" by fishermen. Modern science has now deposed gut and nylon has become the fisherman's favorite. Surgeons have used silkworm gut in surgical procedures for years and still use it for certain conditions.

The breeding of silkworms may have begun in prehistoric times, but the ancient Chinese are generally credited with the first silk-culture (seri-culture) for it is known that the breeding of silkworms and weaving silk flourished in China during the Shang Dynasty (1523–1027 B.C.) and that it was the ladies of the Emperor's Court who first cultivated the silkworms, tended the cocoons, and collected the silk strands for weaving.

Silk became the basis of the earliest trade between China and the Mediterranean, and was a major element in ancient Chinese economy and used as a form of currency. History and legend tell of the 3,000 mile "Silk Route" across Asia between China and Rome. A few silk fragments, excavated a Lou-Lan, an ancient Chinese frontier station, seem to prove that this commerce did exist.

It is hard to believe, but true, that centuries after silk fabrics were being imported from the Orient and used in Europe, silk was believed to be a "fleece" from the seed-pod of the "silk-cotton tree"; some insisted silk fibers were spun by a spider or beetle. Actually, it was not until two Nestorian monks living in China hid silkworms in their *palmer staves* and smuggled them into Constantinople that the mystery was finally solved.

Seri-culture spread rapidly through the Balkan Peninsula, and Byzantine silk became prized for ecclesiastical vestments.

In the 8th and 9th centuries, looms and methods of weaving silk were improved in Greece and Syria, but it was the Greeks who maintained supremacy in Europe until A.D. 1204, when the Latin Empire was established.

Silkworms were first successfully raised in France in the reign of François I (A.D. 1515–1547). In the 17th century, Henri IV, regal patron of the arts, founded and developed the great silk factory in Lyon, France. Cardinal Richelieu, the shrewd Prime Minister who ruled France with an iron hand, loved and collected ribbons. In 1632, he put his entire collection of ribbons into seven volumes and had them bound in green leather. These books can be seen in Paris, and the story of the looms of France is revealed when the pages are turned displaying these bright samples.

Silk weaving spread rapidly throughout Europe. French Huguenots who had settled in England tried unsuccessfully to manufacture silk until a new method of weaving was introduced in 1718. English silks soon replaced French silk in the European market, but the silk industry in France was revived during the Napoleonic and Restoration periods.

Development of silk-culture in the United States began early in American colonial history. In 1609, King James I sent silk worms to Virginia, but unfortunately the ship was wrecked off Bermuda. Four years later, another shipment arrived safely in Jamestown Harbor. Because the silkworm prefers mulberry leaves, the Virginia House of Burgesses immediately passed a law that 10 mulberry trees be planted on every 100-acre plot of land. A fine was imposed for neglect of this duty, but a premium was paid for every pound of silk produced. However, silk-culture was not successful with the colonists.

Today, beautiful pure silk fabrics are being produced in India and in Thailand.

CARE OF SILK

The cleaning of silk fabrics such as brocades, damasks, velvets, and taffetas by amateurs can be disastrous and replacement more expensive than the cleaner's bill. So, in this book, we prefer to avoid instructions on washing or dry cleaning of silk textiles. All that can be done here is to warn the reader that fabrics that appear to be pure silk often contain

synthetic fibers that might disintegrate under a hot iron or when subjected to certain chemical solvents in dry-cleaning products.

The term "dry cleaning," which is so commonly used, is a misnomer,
because fabrics when dry cleaned are subjected to *chemical wetting*, rather
than washing with water.

Dry-cleaning is a highly developed science. Before a fabric is cleaned,
a test is made to determine the types of fibers in the material and what
caused the stain. With this analysis, the technician decides what chemicals to use. If the stain cannot be removed without harming the fabric, a
responsible dry cleaning company will refuse to clean the item.

My best advice is to always discuss cleaning problems with someone
who knows the business.

Pure silk fabrics are rare today. However, we are fortunate to live in an
age of simulated silk. It is not as subtle, but it is safe to wash, dries in a brief
time, is comfortable to wear, and requires no ironing. Drapery and upholstery materials can still be had in pure silk, but as with clothing, the trend is
to combine the pure fiber with blends of synthetic fibers.

Articles made of silk are marked 100% pure silk. If other threads
are combined, they will be named on the label.

Pure silk is difficult to maintain

Silk wrinkles easily and shrinks when washed. Patience and care are
needed when ironing. Never use a hot iron on silk—moderate heat is best.

Water will spot silk, leaving a "ring" that is hard to remove. Have the
garment dry-cleaned.

Spot-cleaning pure silk fabrics can be disastrous! Have the entire item
dry-cleaned. It is the safest method.

Because they are organic, pure silk materials react to excessive dryness
and intense sunlight. The fibers crack and split in areas of low humidity.
Watch the relative humidity in overheated rooms.

LINEN

Linen, one of the oldest known textiles, comes from flax, a slender
erect annual herb that blooms with the loveliest of blue flowers.

Where or when the usefulness of flax fiber was discovered is a secret
buried in antiquity but fragments of linen cloth have been excavated
from damp, prehistoric sites in Europe that appear to be products of the
Neolithic Age.

The cultivation of flax requires manual labor, and the process of turning its strong lintless fibers into thread is very complicated. Flax, fibers, sometimes a yard long are drawn from the plant, then spun into fine threads to be used as *thread* or woven into linen cloth.

Linen is difficult to dye, but it is washable and can be bleached to a lustrous, brilliant white; furthermore, linen is absorbent. A drop of water on cotton remains a long while, but a drop of water on linen cloth speedily disappears. This test was used for many years to rate the distinction between the two fabrics, but modern methods of treating cotton now necessitates a miscroscopic examination of the fibers. Flax fibers are bamboo-jointed, and cotton fibers are twisted, as a rope.

History emphasizes the fact that linen was the chief textile of ancient Egyptian civilization, that it was a luxury fabric, and an article of export. Large quantities of fine Egyptian linen has been preserved on mummies; 300 yards were used to wrap the deceased, and some of the earliest wrappings date from 5000 B.C.

Linen fabrics were manufactured in Flanders in the 7th century. It was Charlemagne (A.D. 742–814) who encouraged the linen industry in France.

The earliest existing examples of linen in the Medieval period are the linen grounds used for the silk and gold embroideries of the Durham Stole and Maniple, and the glorious Bayeux embroidered tapestries, depicting events in the Norman invasion of England. They were done by Queen Mathilda and the ladies of her court while waiting for her husband, William the Conqueror, to return from wars.

In those days, linen became the chief fabric for undergarments, sheets, etc. because it was so easily washed, and its popularity continued until the 18th century when cotton was brought to Europe from India.

In Europe, linen thread was originally woven into narrow strips and these strips all had colored threads woven into the selvedge; the colors used were the trademarks of the weaver. Even today, narrow linen strips are commonly used as dish towels and display the same decorative selvedge. But linen thread was used not only on the loom; it was worked into miracles of loveliness by the fingers of the lace-makers of France and Italy.

When embroidered linen and linen lace was made into "table-linen," it became the vogue, but this beautiful handiwork was scarce;

in France, Louis XV (1715–1774) had no table-linen for the palace so he rented what he needed!

TABLE LINENS

The discovery of needles in the relics of Swiss lake-dwellings shows primitive peoples were acquainted with stitching. Embroideries of unique interest have been found that date back to Ancient Egypt. Romans designated embroidery as "painting with needles." Lace developed with the application of fine stitches on linen and is a descendant of embroidery.

It is believed that Catherine de Medici, wife of Henry II, was the first to import embroidered net and cut-work from Italy and Flanders for use as table-linen in France. She also encouraged the use of lace. In the late 16th century Henry IV wanted to establish lace-working in France but gave up when his Minister of Finance told him, "Sire, you need soldiers and iron, not lace."

CARE OF LACE

Fine lace such as heirloom wedding veils, lace cloths, lace fans— in fact, any lace treasure—should be cared for by an expert skilled in the preservation of lace. Consult with an expert on storing lace.

Very fine lace cloths or doilies should also be tended by experts in hand-laundering.

Tips on washing lace

Lace that edges napkins, doilies, tea cloths, etc. needs special handling after washing. While the lace is damp, with the thumb and first finger of both hands, gently work the lace into shape. If correctly worked or pulled into shape, lace rarely needs ironing.

Warning: Never iron damp lace before it is worked into shape. If you do, it will contract under the heat of the iron and lose its lacy quality.

EMBROIDERED LINENS

Embroidery contracts when wet, so before wetting or washing table-linens, measure one piece of a *set* to know how to shape it before ironing.

1. Spot washing can often eliminate washing an entire article.
2. Soak articles in cold water before washing; hot water sets stains.

3. Wash fine linens in warm water using a mild soap.

4. Wash, then rinse thoroughly to make sure the cloth is free of soap. Soap causes brown stains when a hot iron touches it.

5. Remove excess water by rolling each piece in terry cloth toweling. Iron while damp.

6. With both hands gently pull and shape the material as near to size as possible. Pinning the corners of the doily or napkin to the ironing board is helpful.

7. If the lace edges the item, gently pull and shape the lace with the thumb and first finger of both hands.

To press embroidered articles:

1. Pad your ironing board heavily and cover tightly with sheeting.

2. Place the embroidery face down on the padding.

3. Make sure all corners are square.

4. Place the iron on one area at a time and press firmly.

Only practice can teach the best method of washing and ironing fine embroidered linens.

COTTON

Cotton is a fluffy mass of white fibers around the seeds of various species of mallow plants and its common name comes from the name of the Arabic plant, Qutun.

The mallow family (Gossypium) includes herbs and shrubs that have been cultivated from time immemorial and are the most important vegetable fibers in the world. In warm sunlit areas such as India and Egypt, many species are perennials, but in the United States it is considered best to renew the plants annually.

Microscopic examination shows "mature cotton hairs to be flattened and twisted, somewhat resembling an empty, twisted fire-hose." This characteristic is of great economic importance, facilitating the spinning of fibers into thread or yarn.

The origin of cotton has never been definitely determined, nor the country where it was first used, but archeological discoveries indicate cotton was being used in India 3000 B.C. to make string and fabrics.

Yarn cotton was originally handmade or made on very crude equipment. In the mid 1700's machines for weaving cotton cloth were invented in England. These inventions were carefully guarded secrets.

No drawings were allowed and workers were forbidden to disclose how the machine operated.

In 1789 Samuel Slater brought his working knowledge of this machinery to the United States, then had the machines reproduced from memory. The first cotton mill in America was built in Pawtucket, Rhode Island, in 1793.

During the 18th century, printed cotton fabrics were imported to France from India. These gay fabrics printed in the "style" of the Near East, became the rage. Fabulous brocades, velvets and damask draperies were replaced in palaces and manor houses by cottons. Weavers put such pressure on King Louis XIV that he ordained no cotton was to be imported to France, nor was cotton to be woven on a French loom. A day after his edict was published his Mistress, The Marquise de Pompadour, appeared at Court in a cotton dress. Cotton and the women of France had won.

The first of these cotton importations was called "Indienne." Then other names of Eastern origin were given to popular cotton fabrics; *chintz*, named for the Persian city of Chiniz was, and still is, extensively used for drapes and upholstery; *calico* came from Calcutta, India. An English merchant, at that time, described calico as a "tawdry, pie-spotted, flabby, low-priced thing made by a parcel of heathens and pagans." This comment didn't stop its popularity. Among these imported textiles were lengths of exquisitely textured cottons, hand-painted in brilliant colors of varied designs depicting exotic fruits, flowers, and birds of India. Other fabrics were ablaze with roses, peonies, carnations, chrysanthemums, anemones or pomegranates.

About 1757 a young German weaver named Oberkampf, who had recently arrived in France, received a letter from a lady stating that her "prized piece of Indienne had been ruined, could he duplicate it for her?" Oberkampf worked day and night with dyes and with the cutting of wood block designs in his little mill, in the village of Jouy, near Versailles. At long last he succeeded, and created for France and the world the new, beautiful cotton fabric, Toile de Jouy.

Toiles were soon produced in many cities; great artists were engaged to make designs that depicted scenes of French activities and history. There were scenes of merriment at court, farmers at work, architectural, even revolutionary subjects.

Marie Antoinette decorated the palace rooms with toiles. These lovely cottons were used as curtains, bedspreads or upholstery to decorate the small homes of the Provinces of France.

After the Revolution, toiles were still popular. When the Emperor Napoleon visited the little factory in Jouy, he was so delighted with the beauty of these fabrics, he took the diamond-jeweled star, which decorated his uniform, and pinned it on the breast of Christophe Phillipe Oberkampf.

THE LINEN CLOSET

The custom of calling household textiles "Linens" dates back many years to when sheets, pillow cases, towels, and tablecloths were made of pure linen. This term is confusing to the novice housekeeper, for the linen shelves are now filled with cotton and synthetic textiles.

In any home a well-stocked and organized *linen closet* is an achievement to be proud of. In order to accomplish this:

1. Fold each article neatly and have a special place on the shelf for each category; sheets in one pile, pillow cases in another, hand towels in another, etc. Table linens should have a spot all their own.

2. Doilies and napkins are more easily handled if cardboard mats are placed between "sets." Cardboard is available in myriads of colors and can be cut any size to fit the doilies.

3. Scented sachets or soaps placed on shelves keep the closet fresh and the *linens* sweet smelling.

Laundering table linens

1. It is unsanitary to wash table linens with soiled bed linens, towels, or clothes.

2. Greasy dish towels and kitchen cloths should be washed separately. Borax added to the first wash cycle freshens and softens materials.

3. A few drops of bleach will remove grease and heavy stains, but use as directed on the label. Do not use bleach of any kind on colored materials or synthetic fibers.

Warning: Never pour pure bleach directly onto cloth. Make a solution of bleach and water before adding to the washing machine or laundry tub.

Laundering sheets

1. Launder white sheets in hot water; colored sheets in warm water.

2. Wash dark or vivid colored sheets separately for the first few launderings until any excess dyes are eliminated.

3. Launder your deep-toned sheets *before using them* to avoid any possible discoloration of your blankets or mattress pads.

4. When using bleach, follow the manufacturer's instructions carefully and be sure to use only the quantity suggested on the bleach label.

5. Launder *cotton-and-polyester blend* sheets the same way as all cotton or other wash-and-wear fabrics. These sheets should, however, be *tumble dried* and removed from the machine as soon as they are dry; otherwise, the heat of the dryer tends to set the wrinkles.

6. For softer, smoother sheets, try using a fabric softener; use every three or four launderings, after rinsing.

Laundering towels

1. Never use commercial softeners on towels. The softener builds up a waterproof silicone finish, which will in time make your towels non-absorbent.

2. Wash all new towels separately before using.

3. Wash white towels in hot water.

4. Wash colored towels in warm water.

5. Follow manufacturer's instructions on the bleach or detergent labels.

6. Terry cloth towels are best fluff-dried; do not iron.

7. Smooth each towel on a table top and fold neatly before placing on the shelf of the linen closet.

STAINS

Although linen and cotton are washable, stains can be hard to remove. Here are a few helpful hints.

Soap can cause stains on linen or cotton. These brown stains are probably "scorch," not rust. Soap that remains in fabric due to improper rinsing will turn brown when touched by a hot iron. Rewash; rinse thoroughly.

Red wine is difficult to remove. Never cover the spot with salt; salt sets stains. Submerge spot in ice water as soon as possible or use ice cubes. Don't give up until the stain is out.

Coffee stains must be removed as quickly as possible with cold water. Continue running cold water through the stain until the area is clear; never use warm or hot water, it will set the stain.

Fruit-juice and tomato products spots should be sponged thoroughly with *cold water* and then rinsed with hot water, or the material can be submerged in a presoak enzyme solution. Wash; rinse as usual.

Chocolate stains must be scraped off and the fabric rinsed in cold water, or use a presoak enzyme solution as directed on container.

Egg stains should be presoaked in cold water using an enzyme formula as directed on package. Wash and rinse well.

Grease, gravy, butter, and salad-oil stains are extremely difficult to remove from linen or cotton. Try warm thick suds on these stains. Rub the fabric between hands and rinse thoroughly in hot water, or try *presoaking spots* with any one of the commercially available enzyme formulas that have grease and oil dissolvers in them. Use as directed on the box.

MAN-MADE FIBERS

At the present time, there are too many man-made fibers to describe individually, and by the time this is being read, there may be dozens more. At present, many of these fibers are commonly used in home furnishings for fabrics, rugs, and carpets, and often, fibers are mixed or blended to take advantage of their best characteristics. Synthetic textiles are a boon to people suffering from allergies, and have also eased laundry problems by practically eliminating ironing and by decreasing drying time.

When discussing man-made fibers with a textile manufacturer, I was fascinated to learn that there were originally *four generic* synthetic fibers, as there are *four natural* fibers. From these four synthetics many fibers have been developed, and manufacturers have given each new synthetic textile a name, but the Federal Trade Commission requires the *generic* chemical name be attached by the manufacturer to all fabrics.

Rayon, the first synthetic developed, was known as "artificial silk."

Nylon came next and was made from a combination of coal tar, air, and water. By chemical and physical means, nylon can be manipulated so that its weight, texture, and "hand," can be varied for use in a scope of fabrics from sheer chiffon to wool-like carpeting.

Orlon is important because it was a major discovery as a substitute for wool.

Polyester began the fabulous era of no-iron fabrics.

Qiana, a fifth generic has now been developed. Because of its soft lustrous texture it may become a substitute for silk.

Glass filaments are being made into fabrics that simulate the softness and suppleness of silk, linen, or cotton. This material is heat resistant, insect-proof, mildew-proof, and stain-proof; however, glass fibers are used chiefly for curtains and casement cloth—not for clothes. *Warning:*

Even though *some* glass fiber materials are washable, never wash such textiles in combination with lingerie, clothes, or table linen. The glass filaments combine with cloth to create serious skin problems. Glass fibers disintegrate under the heat of the dryer.

Stretch fabrics are new and being used for furniture covers. Great care must be taken in cleaning, the material can lose its elasticity. Discuss cleaning *stretch fabrics* with an experienced dry-cleaner.

Imitation leather is a beautiful and useful material for all kinds of upholstery, indoors or out.

ULTRA SUEDE

Ultra Suede is the manufacturer's trademark for a fabric imitation of animal-skin suede.

This fabulous fabric is washable, does not shrink or fade, and is being used for dresses, coats, shoes, handbags, upholstery, even wall coverings. The fabric comes in exquisite colors and is available by the yard.

Ultra Suede is washable and dry-cleanable, but *remember these cautions*:

Never use bleach or bluing.

Wash alone to prevent stains from other materials.

Never wring, twist, or towel dry.

Read manufacturer's instructions.

Cleaning instructions

The best method for cleaning Ultra Suede is machine washing. Set dial on delicate cycle. Use warm water and mild soap or detergent, such as Ivory Snow or Woolite.

To tumble dry set dryer dial on permanent press, but *caution*: ten minutes is usually enough time for drying a dress or skirt. Overdrying ruins the fabric. *Never allow article to remain in dryer after it is completely dry.* Remove it at once.

To hand wash Ultra Suede, use warm water and mild soap or detergent. Place on hanger to dry. *Refer to cautions before washing.*

Brush fabric only if necessary to restore suede texture.

Press article, if needed, on the reverse side. Cover with a clean cloth; set iron on synthetic or low heat.

TYVEX-SPUN BOND

Tyvex-Spun Bond is the manufacturer's trademark for a new and interesting fabric. When using this fine material, carefully read the manufacturer's cleaning and care instructions.

The list goes on and on. We should be grateful to the industry for developing such useful textiles but be cautioned. When buying anything from clothes to home furnishings always inquire as to the fabric's potentials, and particularly, how to clean or wash it. If you fail to get such detailed information about its usefulness and get into trouble, don't blame the merchant or the manufacturer, the fault will be yours.

Basketry

BASKETS are made of organic materials and have to be protected and never allowed to become completely dry.

One authority who owns a fine collection of American Indian basketry suggests sponging the materials with a solution of:

40% Castor oil
60% Alcohol

Wipe off any excess solution with a soft cloth.

WICKER FURNITURE

Wicker furniture is made of either reed (cane), rattan (bamboo) or willow. All are natural organic materials.

Wicker furniture whether varnished, unvarnished or painted has to have a good hosing once or twice a year to remove accumulated dust and soot. Also to prevent the fibers from becoming dry. If necessary wash with soap or detergent, hose throughly and wipe off excess moisture. To complete the drying process place the furniture in the sun.

When completely dry the furniture can be revarnished or re-painted. Synthetic varnish is available in three finishes either mat, egg-shell or gloss. Apply carefully and allow the varnish to dry in the sun.

Marine spar varnish is an excellent protective for wicker furniture or baskets.

To paint wicker use any fine paint and apply a thin coat.

Ceramics

SOME of the most beautiful and useful items in the home are porcelain (chinaware), stoneware or earthenware, and all are varying forms of ceramics, commonly called pottery.

Ceramic derives from the Greek word *keramos*, meaning a clay vessel; pottery comes from the Latin *potum*, or pot, and until this highly industrialized age, all ceramics were products of the potter. Except where clay was not available, every culture since the Stone Age has had its potters.

In the earliest stages of ceramic art, the potter's fingers were his only tools; how long ago some genius invented his wheel may never be known, but the potter's wheel ranks among man's earliest and most important mechanical devices.

Though legends, stories, and poems about the potter and his wheel are as old as mankind, the true history of his art is buried in the past because his methods were jealously guarded secrets. We surmise that primitive man discovered clay, used his hands to mold it into any desired shape, then found that by exposure to the sun's heat, the clay became hard. The next step must have been the use of fire to further harden the clay at high degrees of heat—thus, the kiln was developed.

Pottery or clayware, as used by primitive peoples, was made of unwashed clay. These crude items were porous, friable, and certainly not usable as containers for foods, liquids, or for storing food. As man's culture progressed and his personal needs increased, he had to use wood or metalware for domestic purposes.

GLAZE

The art of glazing ceramics began thousands of years ago in Egypt and was perfected in China, Korea, and Japan.

During the Shang Dynasty (1523–1028 B.C.) Chinese potters found that Kaolin—a fine, white clay—fired at very high temperatures became translucent and extremely hard. They also stumbled on the fact that *kiln ash* and *mud* vitrified under intense heat and that a *glassy* coating became fused to surfaces of fired clay. This coating, or glaze, rendered earthenware non-porous and non-absorbent and thus pottery became useful for domestic purposes. The Chinese believed the use of this easily cleaned ceramic would deter pestilence, food-poisoning, and disease. Through the years, this glazed pottery has become known as Stoneware and is the immediate ancestor of Porcelain.

It is interesting to note the terms used to differentiate glazed surfaces: *shining, opalescent, crackled.* In the last case the surface of a ceramic piece is covered with a network of tiny fine cracks that may not be the result of misuse or age but rather are created intentionally. Glazes derive their names from the ingredients used: salt, tin, or lead. They may also be named by color: green, mirror (black), or yellow; or by method of application: liquid, dry, or blown.

Painting ceramic objects is done either under the glaze, in the glaze, or over the glaze. Methods of decorating the glaze include slip, pigment, tooling, turning, incising, relief work, mold, sprigged, and applied.

JAPANESE CERAMIC CULTURE

Japanese ceramic culture did not originate in Japan. Their great knowledge and technique came originally through ancient Chinese and Korean influences. Japanese emperors, recognizing the potters' avid desire to emulate the great ceramic products of other Oriental countries, sent their best potters to China and Korea to study and then return to Japan to teach the fabulous techniques of Chinese and Korean art.

The Japanese potters began by imitating, but soon developed their own techniques, designs, and remarkable glazes. Although Chinese ceramic art perhaps surpasses all others, the Japanese attained a zenith of perfection in pottery and glaze that has rarely been copied.

Very few ancient Japanese ceramics are available for purchase today because these beautiful pieces, developed on the potter's wheel in Japan, have been zealously guarded, generation after generation, and consequently, remain in Japan. It is interesting to note here that ancient Japanese potters rarely, if ever, made designs in pairs, so beware of any dealer who tells you he has an ancient pair of Japanese bowls, figures, or vases.

PORCELAIN

The history of porcelain is very involved, but its development should be regarded as the *evolution* of a product, rather than as a *sudden discovery*.

The term *porcelain* apparently began in Italy, and is the complex derivation of words describing a sea-shell, whose form resembled a pig's back (porc), and whose surface skin was as smooth, opaque, and without perforations, as the new ceramic product.

According to the Encylopedia Americana, *porcelain* is a type of pottery; "white, translucent, hard, heat resistant, and chemically inert the bond between the body and glaze is close and often indiscernable. Porcelain is readily worked by all known pottery methods, is adaptable to every form of ceramic decoration, and differs from stoneware because of materials used and the refinement of the product."

The ancient Chinese described their porcelain as a thin ceramic ware of a hardness that could not be scratched with a knife, was covered with a transparent coat of glaze to give a shining smooth appearance and produced a musical sound when struck with a fingernail.

All accounts seem to justify the belief that porcelain had its beginning in China in the 9th and 10th centuries, during the T'ang Dynasty, and that it was a *porcelaneous* type pottery that was something between stone-ware and true porcelain. This beautiful ceramic was known as Yao in China, and later as *proto-porcelain* in Europe.

In China under the Ming Emperors the demand for yao broke all bounds; houses were roofed with yao tiles, and entire pagodas were made of stoneware and yao. Vases were six feet high, fish bowls large enough for children to play in, statues and deities were larger than life-size. Yet, at the same time, the potter created the most delicate tiny porcelain cups and boxes, no bigger than a coin.

To emphasize the vastness of China's porcelain industry at this time in history, a French missionary who visited Ching-Te-Chen in A.D. 1712, wrote "a million persons live in the city and all are connected in some way with the porcelain industry. When a piece comes out of the kiln it has passed through the hands of 70 workmen."

In the year A.D. 1544, records show the Imperial Household ordered for its use, "26,350 bowls with 30,500 saucers to match, 6,000 ewers with 6,900 wine cups, 680 large garden fish bowls, and 1,340 table services of 27 pieces each!" This output of porcelain was exclusive of world export trade.

When the Chinese Court or any important Chinese family went into mourning, all porcelain dishes and vases used had to be white, the color for mourning.

Early in the 1600's, the Dutch East India Shipping Company began importing this beautiful Chinese pottery to Europe where it immediately became known as "Chinaware." The demand for "China" was so great that European potters tried to imitate it, but without success. If a potter found usable materials, he lacked the techniques for production, and the Chinese would not reveal their methods. The pottery that was made in the 17th century in Europe became known as *soft-paste*, and was particularly important to the French and Dutch ceramic industry.

Enormous quantities of Chinese yao continued to be imported into Europe until the beginning of the 18th century, when large deposits of Kaolin clay were discovered in Saxony. In 1708, a young alchemist, Johann Frederick Böttger, living in Meissen, made a true *hard-paste* pottery. Recognizing this important advance in European ceramics, Augustus I, Elector of Saxony, forbade the exportation of kaolin to other potteries, and imposed secrecy on Böttger and all who knew the manufacturing processes, enforcing his rules with threats of punishment and virtually holding them prisoners in the Meissen fortress, where Böttger was doing his research.

The Meissen factory was immediately founded in Germany and Böttger's methods spread rapidly across Germany into France, England, Holland, and other European countries. Many of the great ceramic factories developed at that time are in existence today.

The glorious porcelains produced in France in the 18th century have never been surpassed and perhaps never will be, for potters, painters, goldsmiths, wood, and metal workers all combined their talents to create lasting works of art.

In our modern world, porcelain is extremely valuable in technology and industry because of its dielectric strength, and chemical resistance to most acids and alkalies. Furthermore, porcelain is weather resistant, and has high compressive strength and stability under abrupt changes in temperature. All *conduits* throughout our American telephone systems are made of this marvelous material that had its beginning thousands of years ago in China.

CERAMIC IDENTIFYING MARKS

Since the beginning of ceramic production, great potters and manufacturers have used identifying marks. Glazers, decorators, gilders, and designers often added their initials or monogram, or some special mark to an article before it was fired to thus identify their handiwork.

These marks on the underside of ceramics, whether old or new, are clues to the authenticity of the product and the value of your possession so, before giving away or selling any marked piece have an expert identify the marks—you may be parting with a valuable object, even though the piece has been repaired or is imperfect.

ANCIENT ORIENTAL MARKS

The curious marks and hieroglyphics used by ancient Oriental potters of China, Korea, and later, Japan often have meanings that relate to the purpose for which the item was intended, or carry a legend, maybe a proverb. More generally, these Oriental characters refer to the date and place of manufacture, such as "Made in the Ch'eng Hua period of the Great Ming Dynasty." Collectors do not place complete reliance on these marks unless they agree with the apparent date of the specimen, for Chinese potters often repeated earlier marks and dates on much later "period" ceramics. Assurance of the authenticity of a piece is available only by consulting an expert.

DISCLAIMER MARKS

Because of pride in their products, disclaimer marks have been used by Meissen and many other factories. Each finished piece was examined; if there was a flaw in the design or glaze, an inspector scratched *two straight lines* through the mark on the bottom of the piece. These lines meant the item was below standard, and the piece, so labeled at the factory, was second grade.

TRADEMARKS

All fine modern chinaware carries the manufacturer's trademark. This is of great interest and importance to buyers because *identifying* marks indicate to the knowing, the quality of the ceramic product.

Original modern porcelain art treasures such as Doughty Birds are made in limited editions. Each piece carries the artist's name and is numbered, therefore making a collection of such ceramic treasures extremely valuable.

The study of ceramic marks and initials is a fascinating facet to the story of the potter's art.

UNDERGLAZE DECORATED EARTHENWARE

This is a beautiful chinaware made by the foremost ceramic companies and is as useful as porcelain but is not to be confused with porous, unglazed pottery. This chinaware may be cared for in the same way as porcelain.

UNGLAZED POTTERY

Unglazed clay, whether baked or not baked, is soft and porous and needs only to be wiped with a cloth or dusted. Since unglazed pottery is rarely used for food or beverages, soap and water washing is unnecessary.

CARE OF FINE CERAMICS

Cleaning porcelain is a meticulous chore and must be done with loving care. This is particularly true of porcelain ornaments that are elaborately decorated with flowers and leaves, or figurines with their exquisite little hands and fingers outstretched. Such delicate *objets d'art* are particularly difficult to clean if dust has been allowed to accumulate for several months or years.

When a ceramic object breaks and needs repair, do not attempt to mend the piece; you may ruin the treasure. Instead, ask a china-shop owner to direct you to a repair artist. Having the repairs done by a professional is worth the expense, because home repairs are easily recognized. A professional told me she struggled unsuccessfully for six months to undo a badly mended piece of porcelain that the owner had glued together with Epoxy. Epoxy is a marvelous product, but should not be used by the amateur to mend porcelain or glassware. Ceramic repair requires highly developed skills and great delicacy of technique.

Dust fine pieces with an artist's paint brush (available at any art supply store) and *never* use a stiff brush or cloth. Delicate decorations will break off and are practically impossible to repair, even if you are lucky enough to find the tiny pieces.

Dust that has adhered to the surface of intricately ornamented porcelains will have to be washed off—dusting would be too dangerous.

When washing delicate ornaments
1. Cover the bottom of the kitchen sink, laundry tray, or a large plastic bowl with a dish cloth or small thick towel, and cover a nearby

table or counter with towels to receive the piece for drying.

2. Fill the sink or plastic bowl with *warm* water, and let me warn you—*never* use hot water. If your treasure has been repaired, the point of glueing loosens and a professional's know-how will be required to mend the broken area—that will be expensive. Furthermore, very hot water can crack the glaze.

3. To the *warm* water, add enough mild soap to make light suds. Add 1 oz. of clear ammonia to every 10 oz. of water—more or less ammonia will not be harmful—the ammonia is used to loosen dirt and give brilliance to any gold or metal ornamentation.

4. Soak the piece a few minutes, remove from the sudsy water, *rinse thoroughly* under flowing warm water from the tap or spray, and place on counter to drip dry. Flat surfaces can, of course, be wiped dry.

5. Make sure all soap and ammonia are rinsed away, for if any ammonia remains on metal ornamentations, the metal will turn green after several days.

Don't put fine porcelain in dishwasher

Never, under any circumstances, put your old, antique, or valued porcelain, such as plates, cups, saucers, etc., in the dishwasher. The chemical soap used for loosening food particles, plus the extreme heat needed for the drying process, will ruin gold decoration and dim or completely destroy color.

Caution: Never use steel wool, soap pads, or any other harsh abrasive when cleaning chinaware.

Chinaware can be stained

Brown stains along cracks or a fine network of hairline discolorations on china indicate the glaze has either cracked, been fractured, or applied improperly.

Coffee cups, teacups, saucers, and pots should be rinsed as soon as possible after using, for if there is an infinitesimal *crack* in the glaze, coffee, tea, and other foods can leave stubborn stains if allowed to remain on china for a prolonged length of time.

Stains can sometimes be bleached by using a solution of any bleaching agent, but I do not recommend this procedure—it's tricky business! Bleaching, unless done by a professional, can destroy gold bandings or color decoration on antique or hand-painted china that has not been fired.

When washing everyday chinaware

1. Remove food particles with a nylon kitchen brush—available at all hardware stores. These brushes have short handles, are sanitary, will not scratch surfaces, and come in colors to match your kitchen or pantry scheme.

2. Rinse the plates in warm water, wash with any well-known liquid kitchen soap, and dry thoroughly with a *clean* dish towel, or place in the dishwasher to do the job.

Dishwasher detergents are not always compatible with the water used in your area. Try various dishwasher products until you find the one that works best on your china, silver, or glassware.

Storing fine china

When stacking plates, protect the glaze by placing round flannel mats between each one; covering the center area is sufficient. Flannel may be bought by the yard and cut into mats to fit the plates.

Hang cups and stack saucers

Whenever possible, hang your cups instead of stacking them.

1. Use plastic covered cup-hooks, screwed into the underside of the cabinet shelf.

2. Arrange cup-hooks to accommodate large or demitasse cups. Space so the rims will not touch; delicate porcelain will chip.

CERAMIC COOKWARE

Ceramic cookware or ovenware should be washed with soapy hot water. Soap-pads, scouring powders or abrasives used to remove stubborn stains will scratch the surface.

Ceramic electric percolators. Once a week after washing your ceramic percolator, fill the pot with water; add 1 tablespoon of baking soda and allow to percolate through one cycle—your percolator will be pristine clean and odorless.

Jade

SINCE prehistoric times, jade, the "Stone of Heaven," has been considered a rare and precious material in China. Highly valued in Chinese tradition as a symbol of wealth and beauty, it was more prized than gold. But none of the world's few sources of jade lie within China's boundaries. The main sources have been the river beds and mountains of Sinkiang, southwest of Mongolia, a caravan journey of 2,000 miles from the center of ancient Chinese civilization, an area that was not always under Chinese control. Other sources of jade, perhaps not even known before the 18th century, were northern Burma and eastern Siberia.

To mine the jade, natives walked shoulder to shoulder in river beds, feeling out the stones with their bare feet. The largest slabs of jade were found on high mountain peaks, chipped away, and sent rolling down the mountainside.

Jade cannot be carved or sculptured, it is too tough to be flaked and too hard to be cut by a chisel. Jade must be ground by abrasive sands carried in an oily or moist condition on tools made of bamboo, wood, steel or iron. Actually, no impression is made on the jade by the tools alone. They act merely as vehicles for the abrasives.

Real jade is cold to the touch. Because of this characteristic any imitation stone is immediately identifiable.

Centuries ago a Chinese scholar wrote: "Jade is possessed of five virtues: *Charity* is typified by its lustre bright and warm; *Rectitude*, by its translucency, revealing color and markings within; *Wisdom* by the purity and penetrating quality of its note when the stone is struck; *Courage*, in that it can be broken but cannot be bent; *Equity*, in that it has sharp edges which injure none."

Jade is easily cared for; wipe the stone with a clean cloth, and remove dust from crevices in the design with a bristle brush. Wash with any mild soap and warm water.

Ivory and Bone

Ivory and bone have both been used since Paleolithic days for varied purposes. Bone, always available in many shapes and degrees of hardness, furnished man with useful implements, such as arrowheads, fishhooks and various tools, but it was also used for ornamentation and carving.

Ivory comes from the tusks of the elephant, walrus, hippopotamus, from whale or sharks teeth, from rhinoceros horn, and the horn of other animals. Ivory is tooth-like in structure and composed of many layers.

Carved ivories exist which date to the earliest Egyptian dynasties and many fine ivories exist from ancient Chinese and Near East civilizations, but the oldest known graphic work on ivory has been found in caves in Dordogne, France and in caves in Switzerland. These tusks, incised with outlines of reindeer and mammoths were done by cavedwellers when elephants roamed Europe.

Ivory is difficult to work with, yet it has been carved, etched, stained, inlaid with metals, semi-precious or precious stones, and is used for veneering.

When carved, the distinction between ivory and bone is difficult to tell by mere inspection. Identification should be done by a specialist.

SCRIMSHAW

This is a delicate form of carving done by incising ivory or shell with special tools and then rubbing ink or pigments into the incised lines to emphasize design.

Some of America's most treasured carvings were made by New England whalers during their long voyages at sea. Scrimshaw is still produced by the fine craftsmen of Cape Cod.

HANDLE WITH CARE

These materials are organic. Both become brittle with age and lose their natural color when exposed to intense sunlight. Display ivory so direct sunlight does not strike the object at anytime. The golden color that ivory develops with age is natural patination. However, coloring may be applied, as is often done by the Japanese carvers of Netsuké.

Ivory, regardless of its age, reacts quickly to sudden changes of temperature and humidity. Under extreme conditions of heat and dampness ivory may suddenly warp or crack.

Dust or wipe old and brittle ivory with extreme care. Use an artist's soft bristle brush.

Caution: if washing neglected ivory becomes necessary to remove accumulated dust or soot, never completely immerse the object in water. Wash quickly, rinse and dry with a soft cloth. Washing old ivory is not advisable.

MINIATURE PORTRAITS

These small portraits are usually painted on ivory. To remove dust wipe gently with a soft dry cloth. A wet cloth could destroy the picture.

Marble

THE name derives from the Greek *marmarien* meaning to sparkle. The best form of marble is a variety of tiny calcite crystals that flash and sparkle in the sun's rays, hence its ancient name.

Marble is a compact rock which in its purest form is composed of carbonate of lime or limestone. The purest marble yet discovered, according to authorities, comes from the Isle of Paros, in the Aegean Sea, and is noted for its waxy quality that gives a statue a beautiful polish. The Greeks were the first civilization to use marble for statuary and bas-reliefs.

Some of the finest marble found in the United States comes from the Rocky Mountains and examples of these marbles can be seen in the State Capitol building in Denver, Colorado.

PACKING AND STORING MARBLE

Choose a storage area where the environmental climate is correct. Never store packed and sealed marble in humid, airless attics or basements: the wrapping paper, straw, old quilts, blankets, etc., are organic and under extremely humid conditions develop fungus spores that will stain marble— particularly white marble.

To emphasize this caution, here is a graphic incident: "A statue of Voltaire, carved by the great sculptor, Rodin, was carefully wrapped in white silk and eiderdown, boxed, then stored where conditions were so damp the wood of the box rotted. When the box was opened, the packing was a mass of old growths and the marble was stained brown, red, and green at all points of contact."

MARBLE FLOORS

Marble floors are beautiful but marble demands special care. Being porous, marble is susceptible to stains and though the surface appears hard, marble is easily scarred by grit, gravel, sand, dirt or other abrasives.

Unfortunately, paste or liquid wax does not protect marble surfaces; it only makes matters worse. Wax collects dirt, shows scuff marks, scratches, and is practically impossible to remove.

Keep marble floors clean.

Vacuum often.

Remove surface spots and dirt with a moist—not wet—cloth or mop. Dry thoroughly.

MARBLE STAINS

Marble is porous, so all stains are difficult to remove. Remember:

Do not use acids on stains, the marble will dissolve!

Try covering the stain with Hydrogen Peroxide U.S.P. 3%.

Allow to "set" for several hours. Repeat if necessary. This method has proven most effective even when professionals said nothing could be done—at least it's harmless!

Moisture from cocktail glasses, flower vases or alcohol leave stains that are often difficult if not impossible to eradicate. Place coasters on the table, then warn family and guests to use them. If you know a marble man who can remove old moisture stains, send me his address!

Oil stains will sometimes yield to a paste made of fine, white Kaolin clay and Benzine. Polish the marble after removing the paste.

Marble, particularly white marble, is subject to *rust stains*. There are several commercial agents to remove rust stains from marble. Use product only as directed.

After the stain is removed, polish the marble with very fine sandpaper or tin-oxide powder on a damp cloth.

To polish marble, use chalk, moistened with a little water and apply friction. But use only on polished, not *honed* or dull finished marbles.

Marble mantles and hearths can be washed with any mild soap and water. Work quickly and thoroughly using a brush to remove dirt from the carving. Rinse by "mopping" with terry cloth towels and clean water. Dry thoroughly.

ALABASTER

1. Dust alabaster with a soft brush.
2. Have a professional clean or remove any stains.

Caution: Never soak alabaster in water. It will dissolve.

Glass

GLASS, according to the encyclopedia, "is one of the first compounds made by man and is the result of combining sand of high silica content and a fluxing alkali—soda or potash, and heated to a high melting temperature, 2800 degrees Fahrenheit." The English word *glass*, comes from the Celtic "glas," describing a bluish-green material.

The Syrians knew the jewel-like beauty of glass 4500 B.C. and excavations in the Euphrates Region have disclosed remnants of glass-furnaces worked by these ancient craftsmen. Sir Flinders Petrie, the great Egyptologist, considered that all glass used in Egypt prior to 1500 B.C. was made in glass furnaces in Syria, for it was not until after this date that Egyptians began making simple drinking-glasses and founded the glass-houses that brought fame to the city of Alexandria.

The earliest known piece of table-glass has been found near Bagdad and is a cylinder of light blue glass "strangely free from flaws." The oldest specimen of Egyptian table-glass is a small goblet ornamented with two yellow bands and inscribed with the name of the reigning Pharaoh (1450 B.C.).

The laborious process used by the Egyptians is too involved to describe here, but it is interesting that priests were consulted before the glassmen lit fires in the primitive hearth pits and that while the ingredients were being fired a ceremonial of noisy incantations was executed outside the glass-house.

Egyptians filled bowls and bottles with food and wine to be placed in tombs for the dead. They also made unguent containers to export eastern cosmetics across the Mediterranean. The art of producing hollow-ware such as dishes, cups and bowls in one operation by pressing glass into open molds was first done by an Egyptian slave 3000 years ago.

The technique of glass-blowing presumably began in Phoenicia 2000 years later. By 50 to 20 B.C. Egyptian glassmen were blowing hollow vessels and shaping them with tools exactly as is done by 20th century craftsmen.

Modern production techniques can find no substitute for the lung-power of its craftsmen and methods of blowing have changed little from those used by the famous glassblowers of Venice 750 years ago.

With the Renaissance came the Venetian, artist-craftsmen to develop the exquisite fragile light weight glass of a smoothness and clarity hitherto unknown. This new glass took color well and tableware could be decorated with filigree work and gilding. Soon these masterpieces of Venice graced every royal table in Europe and were in demand wherever expensive glass could be afforded.

The Grand Council of the Venetian Republic granted liberties and rights approaching nobility to these glassmen. Fearful of foreign spies, the operatives were 'exiled' to the island of Murano in the Adriatic Sea to guard trade secrets and thieves were punished by long terms of imprisonment or death at the hand of a trained asassin. The glass-works of Murano still functions.

Crystal—lead glass—was first made in the 17th century in England. This new glass had a bell-like tone when tapped, and great strength and lustre. Fine crystal has always been handblown, never machine made, and is valuable because no two pieces are exactly alike.

CARE OF ORNAMENTAL GLASS

Antique glass is brittle and must not be subjected to extremes of temperature, so when displaying fine glass keep it away from heating and air-conditioning units.

Sunlight enhances the beauty of glass and does no harm, but *moisture* is its worst enemy. Be careful not to store glass in moist areas.

Rarely used glass, whether displayed in cabinets or stored, must be washed several times a year if it is to sparkle. Dust and grime build up to invite corrosion.

1. To wash glass, add ¼ cup of clear ammonia to a sinkful of warm, *not hot*, water. Soak for a few minutes to loosen dirt particles, then rinse carefully.

2. For extra sparkle, try a little vinegar in the rinse water.

Warning:

1. Towels used for drying glass must be *absolutely dry. Moist* cloth clings or sticks to glass. The drying motion twists the surface, thereby increasing the danger of snapping the bowl, the stem, or both!

2. Never put fine glassware in the dishwashing machine. The extreme heat plus the washing agitation can break the glass.

PROBLEMS OF GLASS

It breaks, scratches, stains and can change color.

Scratches

Don't try to remove scratches on old or new glass. Using harsh abrasives, steel wool, emeryboard, etc. only makes the condition worse. Have an expert use his wheel for effacing scratches or cuts.

Chips and cuts

Don't throw away glasses with slightly chipped edge or cut. An expert can polish or grind off the edge and you will have a usable glass.

Color

Glass left for months or years in direct sunlight changes color because of the sand or other ingredients used when the glass was made.

The coloring is often very beautiful. I have some cheap glass ashtrays that have been used for years on garden tables. Once they were clear white; now they are a beautiful yellow, others are deep purple.

Glass "sickness"

Antique decanters or bottles are sometimes stricken with glass "sickness," a cloudy or frosty condition indicating perhaps that wine has been in the container too long. This "illness" can be remedied, at least temporarily:

Mix fine clay or sand with either water or denatured alcohol, then swish it around in the container until the blur disappears. If this remedy fails and your glass is valuable, see an expert.

Crusty sediments

Crusty sediments that can't be dislodged from bottles by ordinary soap and warm water may yield to a soaking for a couple of days in a mixture of vinegar and water, or washing-soda (sal-soda) and water. The sediment will usually yield to either the acid, or the alkaline bath, depending on what caused the crusting.

WASHING TIPS

1. Glasses used for serving *milk* should be rinsed in *cold water* before soaping. *Hot water* cooks the milk to the glass surface, making it difficult to clean.

2. Babies' bottles and serving dishes that have contained milk, should be thoroughly rinsed in cold water before washing or placing in dishwater.

If you use a dishwasher, everyday glass washed in this modern convenience may become clouded by a dishwashing detergent that is not compatible with the water in your area. Try new products until you find the one suited to your water content.

TO REMOVE GLASS STOPPERS

Removing a glass stopper that is stuck in the neck of a bottle, is delicate business. Don't tap the stopper or the neck of the bottle; you will probably break one or the other. Instead:

1. Run hot water over the neck of the bottle for a short period. This should loosen it. When removing the stopper remember not to twist it. The friction only tightens it.

2. A professional recommends applying a mixture of:

½ teaspoon alcohol
¼ teaspoon glycerine
¼ teaspoon common table salt

3. Cover the entire stopper and neck of the bottle with the mixture. Allow to soak for a few hours.

4. Gently tap the stopper and remove it by lifting.

5. Rinse the stopper and the bottle in clear water. Dry both bottle and stopper thoroughly before returning the stopper to the bottle.

6. Never twist or push the stopper into the neck of the bottle; the friction created causes the stopper to tighten in the opening of the bottle.

Crystal chandeliers, wall brackets and candelabra are kept clean by wiping with a cloth or cotton moistened with alcohol or a strong solution of clear ammonia and water. Whether old or new, handle with great care when washing or wiping because the metal wires that hold the crystals together may break if twisted.

There is now a spray formulated to use on crystal that will clean, then drip-dry.

Discolored light bulbs detract from the brilliance of crystal fixtures and though they give a faint glow, replace them with sparkling new bulbs.

MIRRORS

Man's earliest mirror was the still water of lakes and ponds. With the advent of metals, polished brass or bronze was used to reflect his image. It was not until the 4th century B.C. that Praxiteles taught the use of silver in the manufacture of mirrors.

"Looking glass," as it was called for centuries, was first made in Venice in 1300 A.D. but it was not until 1673 that it was introduced into England.

The first mirror known to have entered France was carried from Italy over the Apennine Mountains on mule-back. This famous mirror still hangs in the Palace of Fontainebleau in the room where Marie de Medici, wife of Henry IV, gave birth to her first son, Louis XIII.

When a method of pouring plate glass was discovered in the early 18th century, the use of mirrors for decoration became fashionable. As the technique of making large mirrors was mastered, "mirror rooms" became the vogue. Entire walls were covered with glistening mirrors. Mirrors were framed into paneling and over mantels, not only to reflect views but to increase the apparent size of the room. This fashion for mirrors reached its greatest point of exaggeration when Louis XIV built the palace of Versailles. Here, the long gallery facing the gardens was lined from floor to ceiling with giant mirrors, and became known as the *galerie des glaces*.

CARE OF ANTIQUE MIRRORS

Antique mirrors are often discolored because the silver backing disintegrates through the years. *Never* resilver the glass, let the mirror enjoy its age and its value, as an antique. If you must see yourself, buy a new mirror in a new frame.

1.   Dust the frame and mirror regularly.

2.   Wipe away accumulated dirt with a soft cloth, moistened with any good window-cleaner or a few drops of household ammonia.

3.   Be careful, don't touch the frame with these products because they could ruin gold-leaf or fine wood frames.

The old superstition about a broken mirror being bad luck goes back hundreds of years. Mirrored glass in those days was expensive and difficult to obtain, so it was really bad luck to break a mirror.

Caution: Every few months, remove the mirror from the wall.

Check to see that the screws holding the wire are firm

If the wire-hanger is corroded, remove and replace. New wire is cheap and it may save an accident.

Check the *backing*. If it is loose, reseal or have new backing applied to keep out moisture, thereby protecting the silver on the glass.

Enamel—Cloisonné

ENAMEL is a hard glass-like substance to which coloring agents in the form of metallic oxides have been added and then fused on to the surface of a metal object.

Cloisonné is a method of enameling that originated in Persia. The word derives from the French *cloison*, meaning a partition.

To make cloisonné, enamel is applied usually to metals—copper, gold, silver, or fine bronze. Very fine metal walls or wires of the same material as the base are soldered by a strong cement to the edge of the metal base, outlining the design. These partitions are filled with vitrifiable enamel pastes of various colors. The work is fired—usually three or four times and enamel added until the surface is approximately level. The enamel is then ground and polished to a high degree.

Handle with care

Any enamel object must be handled gently. Wash with warm water and mild soap, rinse and dry. Never use abrasives or cleaning powders on enamel.

CARE OF ENAMELWARE COOKING UTENSILS

Wash enamelware pots or pans with soapy, hot water and rinse clean.

Warning: do not use scouring powder, soap pads or any abrasive on enamelware. Abrasives scratch the glaze and stains are then inevitable.

Enamelware coffee stains and the stale odor of the oil of coffee are difficult to remove.

1. Wash the pot with soapy, hot water and rinse.

2. Add one or more tablespoons of baking soda; completely fill the pot with water and let stand several hours. Rinse and dry. With this method stains will not develop and the odor of stale coffee will be eliminated.

Stained enamelware pots and pans can be cleaned:

1. Fill container with water then add:

¼ teaspoon of any dishwasher detergent.

1 drop of liquid kitchen soap.

2. Place over heat and allow to simmer three or four minutes.

3. Rinse thoroughly.

Warning: Use as directed, do not add more soap or detergent.

Gold

Gold, one of the rarest of all metals, has been taken from earth for more than 6,000 years, yet the history of gold is difficult to trace. It is, in fact, impossible to set an exact date in terms of years when prehistoric man was first attracted to native metals such as gold, but ever since he discovered the yellow nuggets glistening in stream-beds and gravels, he has wanted to possess gold. Man has slaved for gold, fought for it, and tried to fake it, because ownership of this rare metal has always given man a sense of superiority and power.

Egypt was the richest gold producing area of the ancient world. Great fields of gold existed from which Egyptian wealth was readily mined and though Egyptian mining techniques cannot be traced in detail, it is clear from surviving evidence that ancient civilizations learned the main principles of metallurgy and gold mining techniques from the Egyptians. But as we read accounts of the methods enforced in Egyptian gold mines during the reign of the Ptolemies in the 2nd century B.C., the glory and power of Egyptian culture is tragically tarnished.

The great historian, Diodorus, wrote " . . . Kings of Egypt collect together and consign to the gold-mines those who have been condemned for crime, and who have been made captive in war . . . sometimes only themselves, but sometimes likewise their kindred . . . Those who have been consigned to the mines, being many in number, and all bound with fetters, toil at their tasks continuously both by day and all night long, getting no rest and jealously kept from all escape. Living in darkness, because of the bends and twists in the galleries, they carry lamps fitted on their foreheads. They contort their bodies this way and that to match the behaviour of the rock. What they hew out they throw down on the floor—all this without pause, under the severe lash of an overseer. . . . There is absolutely no consideration nor relaxation for sick or maimed, for aged man or weak woman; all are forced to labor at their tasks until they die, worn out by misery, amid their toil. . . ."

Diodorus summarized the story of gold when he said, "Nature herself makes it clear that the production of gold is laborious, the guarding of it difficult, the zest for it very great, and its use balanced between pleasure and pain."

Gold is a soft lustrous metal, yellow in color, highly ductile, and remarkably malleable. Because of these innate characteristics, gold can be worked into any object, no matter how delicate or massive, and once formed into a work of art, does not tarnish or corrode and is virtually indestructible under natural conditions.

GOLDEN TEXTILES AND "LEAVES"

Gold is so highly ductile that one grain can be drawn into a fine wire measuring 600 feet long, and one ounce of gold can be drawn into a thread that will extend fifty miles. These fine threads, woven into cloth or combined with gossamer silk, create glorious golden textiles.

Even when cold, gold is so malleable it can be hammered into incredibly thin 'leaves.' Hundreds of years ago, Pliny the Elder recorded that an ounce of gold could be beaten into 750 leaves, measuring 4 fingers each way. Methods of hammering gold have been so improved through the years that today, a *troy ounce* (the accepted measure of gold) can be beaten into a film 1/282,000th of an inch thick that would cover approximately 100 square feet and show light through it.

Delicate leaves of so-called 'gold tissue' have always been protected by placing very thin sheets of paper between the folds; from this usage, the common term tissue paper has evolved.

PURE GOLD AND ITS ALLOYS

Gold, being nearly as soft as lead to be workable must be alloyed with another metal, so the term carat is used to indicate the quantity of pure gold in alloy. A carat is 1/24 of the total weight. If a piece of gold is marked "18 carats," it means eighteen parts pure gold to 6 parts of the alloying metal, and so on down the scale.

Copper and silver are the most commonly used alloys with gold, but today, goldsmiths use various alloys to produce gold of varying colors to enhance jewelry or other golden objects.

White gold is alloyed with silver.

Red gold is created by using copper.

Green gold is due to an admixture of silver.

Blue gold contains iron.

Purple gold, a modern color, is created by alloying gold with aluminum.

ANCIENT COINAGE

Gold and silver coinage came into being in Asia Minor when Croesus, the richest ruler of ancient civilizations, had gold and silver made into coins, and each coin stamped with his royal device, facing heads of a lion and a bull. Gold and silver coinage, thus devised thousands of years ago, became the foundation on which the economy or political power of modern civilizations have prospered or fallen.

THE WEDDING BAND

In Medieval days, gold crowns, circlets, rings, and jewels worn by royalty and the nobility were used not for ostentation, but as a means of safeguarding personal wealth. At a later period in history when only royalty or the nobility was allowed to use gold coinage, the less wealthy wore gold rings to secure their small fortunes. In time, the gold ring became the wedding band, a symbol signifying the bestowal of wealth from a man to his bride and the sharing of worldly goods.

GILDING

GILDING means to cover any surface with gold and is done by several methods.

Gilt bronze (*bronze d'oré*) is a method of gilding bronze that was used extensively in France in the 18th century to mimic gold and give an impression of richness to any decorative scheme.

Bronze, at this time, was considered the best metal base to use for gilding metal. Its close-grained texture and strength made it suitable for ornamentation on furniture or to support and strengthen fragile objects.

The gilding process was done by covering a bronze, or any metal form, with an amalgam of *gold* and *mercury*. This special formula, called Mercury-Gilding, was spread over the metal and heated, the mercury was thus driven off as vapor and a coating of gold was left in an absolutely pure state on the surface of the metal.

Benvenuto Cellini, in his *Treatise on the Goldsmith's Work*, discusses this process of mercury-gilding in detail and tells that the fumes, resulting from the heating process, were extremely poisonous and advised the sculptor to "leave this work to someone else." This method of mercury-gilding was banned by law many, many years ago.

CARE OF ANTIQUE GILT BRONZE

Time may dull the golden lustre of gilt-bronze. To restore its brilliance is difficult—only a goldsmith with great expertise should be allowed to work with bronze-d'oré. Regilding could devaluate a rare piece.

Don't allow dust or soot to accumulate. Use a small stiff brush to clean the intricate designs.

Water, with a few drops of household ammonia added, will not be harmful if all ammonia is completely rinsed off. Dry thoroughly.

VERMEIL

Vermeil, a French word, describes silver that has been gilded. During the early 18th and 19th centuries vermeil was made in many countries but some of the greatest pieces were made in France by the mercury-gilding process.

Modern silver-gilding is done by an entirely different method.

Vermeil should be washed with soap and water and dried with a soft cloth. Never use polishing agents or abrasives of any kind.

GOLD LEAF AND GOLD FOIL

Gold leaf is also used for gilding many surfaces but is particularly suitable for covering wood surfaces.

Gold leaves vary in thickness from 1/200,000 to 1/250,000 of an inch.

Gold foil is much thicker than gold leaf.

Care of gold leaf

Any surface that has been gold-leafed is valuable. Frames of old mirrors or pictures have often been gilded with gold leaf. Care is simple: check the environmental climate and keep the object free of dust or soot. Use a soft brush for dusting.

The application of gold leaf is difficult; only an expert should repair any damage or peeling.

Caution: A cloth or the vacuum cleaner could remove any loose particles.

GOLD JEWELRY

CARE OF JEWELRY

Gold, if reasonably pure, does not tarnish, but jewelry may become dull, and should have its pristine brilliance restored before wearing.

You will hear that jewelers boil valuable jewelry to cleanse and restore brilliance, but I cannot advise the amateur to use this method. A well-known jeweler tells me a client brought him a "glob" of metal and precious stones that was once a piece of jewelry. While boiling her jewelry, the client answered her telephone and forgot the pot was still on the stove; the water boiled out of the pot, leaving a shapeless metal mass embedded with precious stones.

Many excellent commercially-packaged agents are available for cleaning jewelry but the following hints are inexpensive and equally efficient for every day care. Cleaning jewelry is a simple procedure.

1. Fill a small bowl with any liquid soap and a teaspoon or more of clear household ammonia—the ammonia adds lustre to the gold and brilliance to any encrusted stones.

2. Immerse the pieces in the bowl; let stand a few minutes.

3. Remove one item at a time.

4. Using a *soft* toothbrush, gently brush the piece and rinse in hot running water.

5. Dry carefully

This formula is equally good for cleaning precious stones set in platinum. (Never wash pearls in anything but clear, cold water. Dry, with a soft towel.)

Warning: Before rinsing, *be sure* to close the drain stopper in the basin, or you may have to call a plumber to retrieve your treasure from the waste-trap.

GEMS AND STONES

Stones of many types in real or costume jewelry are popular at present and need special care when being cleaned.

Because there are lovely gems and stones and to recommend how to care for each one would be lengthy and involved, I suggest you have a jeweler or gemologist identify any particular gem or stone and advise you on how best to clean it.

Silver

Collecting silver can well become a fascinating hobby, but I warn you that all you need to do is inherit one piece of fine antique silver, or buy a beautiful piece you see in an antique shop, and you are hooked! From then on you search and acquire what your pocketbook allows—sometimes it doesn't allow! If you can't afford an antique, don't be discouraged. There are excellent sterling silver copies and magnificent Sheffield plate. All that is missing will be the patina of age and the hallmark. So gently polish your newly acquired modern treasure, it will soon acquire its own patina and give you untold pleasure and service.

Any one who refuses inherited silverware, or brides who specify "no silver gifts" because it is difficult to clean, are indeed denying themselves and their families great pleasure. Silver is a good investment. Silverware is easily washed and quickly polished, and although silver will dent or bend through careless use, it never chips or breaks.

Silver, being strongly resistant to atmosphere, oxidation, and most organic compounds common to foods and beverages, is extremely useful in the home and outlives the finest china. Silver flatware, bowls, serving trays, tea or coffee services, candlesticks, etc., are utilitarian as well as beautiful, and certainly enhance the elegance of home surroundings.

The history of silver uses and silver crafts, like furniture, have followed the great influence of conquest and culture, so we trace here briefly some highlights of its story, hoping the reader will appreciate more fully the uses of this lustrous metal and the craftsmen who have handled it with such ingenuity.

Silver, the whitest of all metals, has been known and used by mankind since the dawn of history, and through the centuries has become a symbol of personal wealth, an influence and monetary balance among civilized nations.

Silver is widely diffused throughout nature and occurs in minute amounts, even in seawater. Legends tell that the ancient Chinese believed silver could be mined anywhere that wild onions were growing. Ancient alchemists attributed the white brilliance of silver to moon-glow and called the metal Luna or Diana, meaning the Crescent Moon. Silver Nitrate is still referred to as Lunar Caustic!

Second only to gold in ductility and malleability, silver readily responds to the silversmith's every whim. Silver is soft, therefore useless unless alloyed with another metal. Copper is the most commonly used alloy.

To control the permissible amount of copper to be alloyed with silver, King John of England, in 1180, created the Goldsmiths' Guild, then entrusted the Guild with the enforcement of silver laws. Each article of silver manufactured had to be assayed and marked by a member of the Guild, and the assay-marker was as responsible as the smith for any piece that did not contain the proper proportion of silver and alloy. Substandard pieces were broken, and the smith severely punished; death could be the penalty. As a matter of history, the gold- or silversmith was a man to be reckoned with and in time became our first banker.

As a further guarantee of the silver standard, all fine pieces of English silver were hallmarked. These marks are invaluable to connoisseurs and collectors of fine silver and a fascinating subject to pursue. Hallmarks identify the silversmith, place of origin, and approximate date a piece was made.

Sterling means a silver alloy of standard quality which is 925 parts *pure silver* and 75 parts copper alloy.

The term undoubtedly originated with early English coins and may have derived from the word *staer* meaning a *starling*, because some of Edward the Confessor's pennies bore figures of *four birds*. However, in the 13th Century, King John brought coiners to England from the Netherlands and the Hanseatic cities to improve the quality of English coinage. These coiners were called Easterlings. Some authorities believe the term Sterling evolved when Easterling was contracted to Sterling.

Little is known of English silver-craft prior to 1660. At this period in history, English and French monarchs and nobility kept their wealth in silver or gold *objets d'art*, not only for their pleasure and use, but as bullion to be melted down as needed to finance wars. In France, during the reign of Louis XIV (1643–1715), some forty ordinances and edicts were issued for the melting down of silver and gold articles, and though the reasons for the Royal edicts were varied, the tragic result was the almost total destruction of France's finest silver and gold pieces. In England, so few pieces survived the austere rule of Oliver Cromwell (1653–1658) that the Coronation of Charles II had to be postponed to allow time for the designing and making of new silver regalia.

After the Restoration, with the return of Charles II to the throne, England's silver-craft began to flourish; 1660 therefore, is considered an arbitrary date for the beginning of the production of England silver as we know it today. Monarchs and wealthy patrons began commissioning goldsmiths to design and produce silver chandeliers, sconces, mirror frames, platters, and tea services, even furniture embellished with silver. It was the Silver Era! When sets of flatware came into style, invited guests were no longer required to bring their own knives and forks.

At the turn of the 18th century, during the reign of George I in England (1714–1727), Paul de Lamerie, one of the greatest of all goldsmiths, fled warring France with his father and other French Huguenots to seek asylum in England. Stimulated by the work of such great artisans, English goldsmiths began to design and produce some of the finest silver pieces of all times. So began the golden age of English silver, commonly referred to as "18th century or Georgian silver."

SILVER PLATE

In the early 18th century, solid silver was owned and used mainly by the nobility and people of great wealth, and did not come within the reach of the middle class family. All this was changed in 1742 when Thomas Boulsover, a cutler working in Sheffield, England, accidentally fused silver onto copper while repairing a broken knifeblade. Boulsover had unknowingly revolutionized the silver trade when he discovered that these two metals, silver and copper, became inseparable when heated. Recognizing the commercial value of his discovery, Boulsover began making articles that had the appearance of solid silver, yet were stronger and cheaper to produce. Now people of modest means could have replicas of solid silver at a fraction of the cost.

By the end of the 18th century, Sheffield silver was being made in quantity and became a leading industry in Britain and the town of Sheffield a manufacturing center of great importance.

In 1838, the Russians succeeded in creating a very fine method of *electroplating silver*; consequently, the older and slower process of Sheffield plating, discovered by Boulsover, died out.

Really old Sheffield articles are beautiful and extremely valuable. If you own any real Sheffield and the pink of the copper begins to show through the silverplate, do not have the piece resilvered. Resilvering would be immediately apparent to a connoisseur and ruin the value of the piece.

AMERICAN SILVER

The history of silver in America begins in Boston in the early seventeenth century. There were many laws governing silver making in America, but the silversmiths were not as rigidly controlled as in England. However, a smith working alone could not use his mark until he was twenty-one. It is good to report that few smiths were ever in trouble with the law! There were no banks or bank vaults in 17th century America. The silversmith was respected, he handled his neighbors' wealth and was trusted implicitly. During this period it was difficult to hide money, so it was safer to have silver coins melted and made into a large teapot than to try to hide a box of coins under the mattress! A teapot or silver piece, unique in design and monogrammed, was almost impossible for a thief to dispose of.

As the years passed, American silver followed style trends. Colonial to Classical, Federal and Empire, then to Victorian and magnificent silverware was created by our craftsmen. Some of the finest examples were made from melted coins and the content was almost the same as sterling.

The English used the terms Silver or Silver Standard (Sterling), but in America, Coin, Dollar, or Standard were more commonly applied to silverware. The term Pure Coin, Warranted Pure Coin, or Warranted, had to be used on *solid silver* pieces when silver-plating became popular in approximately 1803. Later, the word Sterling was adopted and is still stamped on silverware, and indicates the piece is .925 per cent pure silver.

By 1840, silverware in America was being made by machine, and the great age of handcrafted silver was ending.

THE SILVER TEAPOT AND CHINA TEA

Early in the 1600's a new beverage, "China Tea" (Teka, as it was called in China), was imported to Holland by the Dutch East India Shipping Company, and soon after imported to England. Because of legends that accompanied tea on its voyage to Europe, credulous Englishmen believed that this new drink had medicinal virtues, for the story goes that the ancient Chinese "drank tea to cure gout, gravel in the kidney, and if drunk after meals, would take away all crudities of the stomach."

Be that as it may, tea immediately became the social beverage as well as a cure-all, and fashionable England needed a silver utensil for serving this delectable drink. So it was that the first English *silver* teapot came into being in approximately 1670.

Care of silver pots
Silver containers designed to serve hot beverages often have ivory, ebony, or wooden handles. Such handles have been used on the finest silver pots for many a year, not only as adornment, but for the practical purpose of insulating the heat that would otherwise be conducted from the pot to your hand.

Ivory or wooden *disks* are also used to insulate handles made of silver. *Knobs* made of ebony, wood or ivory are used on lids for the same reasons.

Extra care should be taken when polishing or washing such pots.
1. Use warm soapy water, rinse thoroughly. Detergents will bleach wood.
2. Dry handles or knobs thoroughly before replacing in a cabinet for storing.
3. Silver polish also ruins wood, ebony, or ivory—so be careful. Occasionally use a small amount of paste wax on such handles.
4. Wax the knobs, too!
Caution:
1. If a pot is dropped, handles loosen, crack, or break off, and these handles are next to impossible to repair or replace.
2. If the handle or disk-joints loosens, have a silversmith replace the tiny silver pins that keep the handle and disk firmly in place. Do not attempt "home repair."

PROTECTING YOUR SILVER
Silver is a soft metal even when alloyed, and the finest silver articles can be bent or dented by careless handling. It is a proven fact that polishing abrasives or friction of any kind used on silver remove infinitesmal amounts of the metal. In time, polishing, rubbing or buffing will completely obliterate crests, monograms, etchings, and worse, render valuable identifying hallmarks indiscernible.

Silver in the home should be used. Daily washing by the natural means of soap and warm water will deter tarnish, maintain brilliance, and in time, create a beautiful patina. But when silver becomes dull or tarnished, it is important to know what to use to restore its lustre, and how to use it. Before discussing what to use to clean silver, let's know what not to do, for the don'ts are more important that the do's.

1. Don't allow a jeweler, or silversmith, to polish your silver by *machine-buffing;* the friction created can wear holes in the metal.

2. Don't rub silver to create a polished surface; an efficient silver cream does the work without rubbing.

3. Don't use *silver-dip* as a short cut to polishing silver; it leaves an unnatural white finish on the silver, and destroys any oxidation put there by the silversmith.

4. Do not use the *electrolytic* method of cleaning silver. It is frowned on by all experts and connoisseurs. This method may be quick and easy, but leaves the surface dull, white, and lusterless, and removes all the beautiful oxidation from the embossing.

5. Never *lacquer silver*. To begin with, lacquer is poisonous and must not touch food or beverages. Furthermore, if lacquer "wears" on silverware or cracks, the exposed silver areas tarnish, and cleaning becomes almost impossible. Lacquer is difficult and expensive to remove, and in the doing, the process steals silver from the surface.

ENEMIES OF SILVER

Foods are some of the worst enemies of silverware in the home. Tarnish develops rapidly from salt, olives, salad dressings, vinegar, eggs, and some meats. Salt and eggs are perhaps the worst offenders.

Silver salt-cellars or dishes used for serving salted nuts, crackers, or highly salted foods must be washed as soon as possible after using. *Salt (sodium chloride)* left on silver creates dark gray dots that enlarge rapidly into pits and unless controlled, eat through metal. As soon as these discolorations appear take the piece to a silversmith—control of this mold is difficult.

Gilding is often used to line salt cellars or bowls to deter salt mold. Abrasive polishing agents will remove protective gold.

Eggs and *recipes containing eggs* rapidly tarnish silver. Tips of forks and spoons have to be cleaned often, and food should be removed as quickly as possible after serving. Wash the silver container and lightly polish before storing. Silver gloves or cloths, used dry, make such cleaning easy.

The egg has its problem, too! Silver tarnishes the yolk of hard boiled eggs.

Flowers and *fruit* may be lovely in silver containers, but they generate acid that can etch the container and cause serious damage. If silver bowls are used for this purpose, use plastic or glass liners, or line the bowl with aluminum foil. Check the bowl daily and remove fruit or flowers at the first sign of decay.

TARNISH AND OXIDATION

Tarnish and oxidation are two different subjects and should be understood before attempting to polish silverware.

Tarnish is a brown discoloration caused by furnace fumes, steam heat, humidity, air-pollution, cigarette smoke, certain foods, or just plain neglect.

Oxidation, the dark gray areas found on embossed silverware, was put there by the silversmith to emphasize design and must not be removed or disturbed by polishing abrasives.

Museums and collectors are now protecting silver from tarnish by using "tarnish-shield," a product that cleans and protects against tarnish in one application. This is not a lacquer or a permanent deterrent to tarnish, and must not be applied to silverware used for serving food or drinks.

Several excellent "tarnish-shields" are available at hardware stores, jewelers, or kitchen departments.

Silver mitts and cloths require no wetting; used when dusting silver they maintain the lustre of ornaments such as:

Cigarette boxes   Jewel boxes
Dressing-table sets   Candlesticks
Silver frames

But again, use gently. Do not buff or polish the silver.

Caution: Do not use *rubber gloves* when polishing silver. Sulphur in the rubber is bad for silver!

Camphor blocks

Camphor gum emanates a protective atmosphere that really deters tarnish on silverware. It is an old-fashioned but effective and easy way to care for silver that is used every day. Available at drugstores or kitchen-ware departments. Place one or more "blocks" in flatware-drawers and on cabinet shelves where silver is stored.

TO CLEAN AND BRIGHTEN SILVER

Use non-abrasive silver foam or silver cream. New polishing agents have replaced the old, highly abrasive products that have been used for too many years.

1. Use a soft sponge or cloth. Never use brushes. Moisten the sponge in warm water, dip into foam, apply lightly to silver surface—do not *rub*—wipe gently.

2. Rinse in warm, flowing water to remove all foam. Do not use soap after polishing, it will destroy the brilliance of the newly polished surface.

3. Wipe dry with clean soft cloth. Allow silverware to dry thoroughly before storing.

Silver mitts and cloths require no wetting; used when dusting silver they maintain the luster of ornaments such as cigarette boxes, jewelry boxes, dressing-table sets, candlesticks, and silver frames. But again, use gently. Do not buff or polish the silver.

Knife handles

Silver knife-handles are hollow; the blade is cemented into the handle. It is advisable to wash these knives by hand—the extreme heat and agitation in the dishwasher can loosen the cement.

Be very careful when washing *knives with handles of porcelain, ivory or bone*.

Stainless Steel and *Diralyte knives* are molded in one piece. However, dishwash detergent can discolor these metals.

Silver candlesticks

Felt is glued to the base of *silver candlesticks* to prevent the metal base from scratching table surfaces, and this felt must be protected from moisture when polishing the "stick."

Use silver-cloths impregnated with silver rouge or tarnish-shield to clean candlesticks. This procedure needs no rinsing, just wiping clean.

If silver cream is used, avoid wetting the base while rinsing the candlestick.

Candlewax can be easily removed by using a soft cloth soaked in very hot water.

Glass or plastic candlewax protectors, called bobeche are inexpensive and available at all hardware stores, gift shops or jewelers. *Dripless* candles are also available.

SILVERWARE WILL BEND OR DENT

Never place a heavy item on any silver piece, not even another piece of silver. For example, if a tray with feet is placed on top of another tray or platter, the feet will leave dents that are expensive to remove and sometimes they can't be removed at all.

Silver *bends* if pressure is applied while polishing. Fork tines and handles of flatware bend. The edges of bowls and trays can be ruined.

Never *stack* chinaware on top of knives, forks or spoons. The weight will bend the handles.

Before each meal: fill a medium size mixing bowl with hot soapy water; as plates are removed from the table, put knives, forks and spoons in the bowl. Scrape the plates and stack. By the time you are ready to wash the flatware or put it in the dishwasher, food particles will have loosened. This little hint saves time, and protects flatware from bending.

STORING CAUTIONS

For *daily protection* or *for storage* of silverware there has never been a finer product than Pacific Cloth. It is available by the yard for lining drawers or cabinets, or, you can buy it in 30- or 36-inch squares. Made into bags to fit special pieces, it gives super protection. Pacific Cloth lasts for years.

Tarnish-shield paper is another great product, but it is not as useful and durable as cloth for everyday use.

Silver, to be stored for a long period of time, should be polished, then wrapped in several sheets of white tissue paper and covered with anti-tarnish paper. Better still, use Pacific Cloth bags for individual pieces. If bags are not available, wrap each object in a Pacific Cloth square.

Never use any self-sealing clear material to store silver. It adheres to the surface, traps moisture, and tarnishes the silver.

Warning: When storing silver for any length of time, under no circumstances place felt or flannel pads between silver trays, platters, etc., and seal with storing paper. *Felt* and *flannel*, being organic, hold moisture that will tarnish the silver surface. Only a professional with a buffing wheel will be able to restore its pristine beauty.

Caution: Plated silver must not be stored in newspaper; the "printers' ink" will, in time, remove the plating.

Copper pieces are often plated with another metal, usually silver, so, remember, some of the plating is removed everytime the piece is polished. Rub gently.

Never use rubber bands; rubber leaves brown stains that even a silversmith finds next to impossible to remove!

Copper

COPPER, a metallic element, was one of the first metals known and used by man. Apparently, copper was plentiful on the earth's surface millenniums ago. Neolithic man used copper and as early as 4500 B.C., developed copper "working" to a high degree. As early as 3000 B.C., copper deposits were worked in Cyprus and centuries later, in Greek and Roman times, these same Cyprian deposits formed a large portion of the world's copper supply.

When Caesar's armies invaded England, Romans referred to the metal as *cyprum; cyprum* was corrupted to *cupreum* from which came the English word, copper. The French word for copper is *cuivre*; German, *kupfer*; and Spanish, *cobre*.

Copper's ability to conduct electricity and heat, its great resistance to corrosion, and its plasticity make it particularly useful in engineering.

There are approximately 3,000 useful commercial alloys used with copper, the principal ones being silver, zinc, tin, nickel, aluminum, cadmium, arsenic, beryllium, and chromium. Brass and bronze are also used, and some of the listed alloys were known and used in the Bronze Age.

CLEANING AND CARE

Because copper is tarnished by the same atmospheric substances that tarnish silver, it needs to be polished often if the glorious pink lustre of the metal is to be maintained.

In this modern age, copper polishing is relatively easy because kitchen departments and hardware stores offer many excellent non-abrasive copper cleaning products.

1. Clean as directed by the manufacturer using a soft sponge or cloth.

2. Wash well in hot water and mild soap to remove the polishing agent.

3. Rinse in hot water.

4. Dry thoroughly and enjoy the beauty of the metal's glow.

5. Never use steel wool, soap pads, or any harsh abrasive on copper

and never under any circumstances, use a buffering wheel to polish copper.

Copper spots
1. Treat spots with a mixture of:
   Hot vinegar and salt;
   Lemon juice and salt;
        or
   Any commercial "copper cleaner."
2. After any treatment, wash the piece immediately with soap and water.
3. Rinse well, dry thoroughly.

LACQUERING COPPER

Having solid copper pieces lacquered may cut polishing time, but the lacquer precludes any chance of a fine patina developing, and once the lacquered finish cracks, the surface will craze, moisture seeps under the finish, the lacquer peels, and the metal discolors. A silversmith can remove the lacquer.

Bronze

'HOUGH the history of metals is not absolute, it is believed ores were iscovered 10,000 or more years ago and that *bronze* was the first alloyed 1etal used by man.

During the Neolithic period when man was learning to produce rticles to cope with his needs, he discovered that by adding tin to opper, a harder, stronger, more easily melted metal could be made. Veapons became more dangerous and tools more useful, when he ·arned the art of casting. Because of the many uses of bronze and its istorical importance in art, archeologists named that epoch between 000-1000 B.C. the Bronze Age.

From the very beginning of the Bronze Age, possession of bronze ›ols and weapons enabled man to subjugate his stone-using neighbor, 1d he believed his power was in the magic of the bronze, and not ithin himself. Thus, bronze underlies the development of a military ristocracy in early emerging civilizations.

Bronze is not just an alloy of tin and copper; it is a "molten alloy ' copper, tin, zinc, aluminum, and other alloys in varying combina- ons," and the term bronze is a French word adopted in the 16th ·ntury from the Italian *bronzo* or *bruno*, meaning brown.

Metal *objets d'art* and utilitarian items are easily cared for because ιey are not subject to biological action, light does not affect them and rocesses that do cause deterioration in metals are slow. The principal ·e is oxidation.

The patina or finish on sculptured bronze is achieved after casting y applying chemicals of colors ranging from black, deep brown, etc., 1d various hues of green, to light gold. These chemicals are used by the ulptor to achieve special finishes and to enhance the texture and beauty ' his work; bronze art objects therefore, must never be subjected to ›lishing abrasives of any kind for they will destroy this patina.

CARE OF BRONZE

Flannel makes good cloths for dusting bronze. Never use abrasives. lean bronze ornaments once a week to avoid accumulation of dust.

To clean bronze that has been neglected and is covered with dust 1d grime:

1. Use a soft brush to remove dirt in crevices and wipe with a cloth

2. If a high gloss is required, dip a flannel cloth in liquid wax, and lightly buff.

Weathered bronze usually darkens. This is natural and does no harm to the piece. However, it should be cared for.

1. After several months' exposure, brush-wash with soap, water and a few drops of ammonia.

2. Rinse; dry thoroughly; apply wax, and buff gently using a clean flannel.

After this treatment, the elements will gradually add a natural patina.

While researching the care of bronze, I learned that the most commonly used wax is a well known neutral shoewax available at all shoe repair shops!

Bronze disease

Bronze disease is a serious problem. It manifests itself in a sudden outbreak of corroding patches, characterized by rough, light-green spots. *Bronze disease* is induced by chlorides and dampness combined with oxygen. Consult a specialist on how to control the "disease."

Brass

BRASS, a copper alloy in which zinc is the principal alloying element in amounts up to 43 percent, is closely related to bronze and has been used continuously since metal alloys were first made in the Neolithic period.

The uses of brass are too numerous to list but because of its beauty and durability, its role in the decorative arts and in the home, brass should be respected and admired. Above all brass at all times must show its glowing yellow lustre and not be allowed to tarnish or become dull.

CARE AND CAUTIONS

To polish brass use any good metal cleaner; there are many on the market. Apply as directed and buff.

Very fine steel wool or fine emery may be used on neglected brass surfaces; then, a polishing agent can be used to create a velvety finish.

Special lacquers are useful for ornamental brasses, but lacquered andirons can become discolored from intense heat.

Caution: When polishing brass drawer pulls, knobs, handles, galleries on tables, etc., do not allow the brass polish to touch the wood, marble table tops, or other materials.

Pewter

PEWTER, a tarnish resistant alloy, has been known and used for domesti utensils since the Bronze Age and, according to the dictionary, is a "combination of various alloys having tin as their principal ingredient." The finest pewter consists of "tin hardened with a little antimony, cop per, and bismuth."

The basic composition of very old pewter was tin and lead. Mor modern pewter has antimony or some copper to replace lead, for pewter debased by undue proportions of lead, is rendered poisonous and unfi for serving acid foods and beverages.

About A.D. 1348 the Pewterers Guild was founded in England t set the rules governing the making of pewter and all laws were rigidl enforced. In 1503 the Worshipful Company of Pewterers was chartere by the Crown and English craftsmen began to mark their wares with "touches" to indicate membership in the guild. Fairly accurate record exist to trace these markers' names, but "touches" are in no way com parable to the hallmarks used by goldsmiths on gold or silver items of th same period.

Pewter at this time was first *cast*, then spun on a lathe and ham mered. The molds used for casting were made of either brass or gun metal, and were so expensive that pewterers passed the molds from sho to shop to defray the original cost.

The earliest pewter used in America was brought from the father land by the colonists and, we asume, was made from those same ex pensive English molds. The story of American pewter begins in 163 when Richard Graves opened his pewterer's shop in Salem, Mas sachusetts.

Unfortunately, posterity has been denied many beautiful items o pewter, both English and American, because being a soft metal, pewter wears out with constant use. As a consequence, the colonists took their worn out pieces to the pewterer to be melted and remade into simple plates and spoons. Some of the finest examples were sacrificed to furnish bullets for two wars.

Much American pewter is unmarked, but if the "touch" mark is used, it is usually on the bottom of a piece, or on the inside of a hollow piece. Faint marks can be brought out by rubbing the area with an ink eraser.

CARE OF ANTIQUE AND MODERN PEWTER

Antique and modern pewter must be handled and cleaned by *entirely different methods*. My best advice on the care of pewter, whether old or new, is to study the subject and advise with professionals.

If you own a valuable old piece of pewter it would be a crime to allow a novice to attempt restoration. Furthermore, pewter develops a "disease" which can destroy the piece if left unnoticed, and only a collector or professional can tell what is needed to cure the disease and protect the piece from further deterioration.

Old pewter likes a warm environment; if left constantly in an area where the temperature drops below 60°F., pewter slowly disintegrates.

Before cleaning pewter, remember, the beauty of old pewter is its dull blue-grey color. Pewter is not supposed to have the lustre and brilliance of silver.

Unless a piece of old pewter is badly oxidized, the dull slate-grey surface will yield to *patient* rubbing with a mild abrasive but, be careful, pewter is very soft. Even the mildest abrasive can create holes in the metal.

It is important to remember, after cleaning or polishing pewter of *any* age, to wash it thoroughly, using a mild soap and warm, flowing water to remove all oil and abrasive. Flowing water rinses any object better than dunking it in a pan of water. When washed, dry carefully, using a clean cloth, and be careful not to leave fingerprints on the clean surface.

Very fine polishes, especially formulated for the care of old pewter, are now available.

To clean old pewter, follow these three steps.

   1. Dust, then wash with any mild soap and warm water.

2. Rinse well. Dry with a clean, soft cloth.

3. When using a commerical polishing product, follow directions exactly.

Another good method is to use a mild kitchen scouring powder moistened with olive oil or kerosene. On stubborn stains, gently rub with very fine steel wool (.0000), or the *finest* of emery powder combined with water or kerosene.

Caution: Lacquering pewter is not advisable if the piece is to be used for serving food or beverages because lacquer is poisonous.

I suggest that *old* pewter should not be used to serve children's meals or drinks; porcelain or silver is best for use in the nursery.

Today's version of pewter is a tarnish-proof alloy, about 90% tin, and requires a minimum of cleaning. Some of our finest silver houses are now making beautiful and useful pewter for the home, and the purity of design blends well with some periods of furnishings.

This lovely *new* pewter should be kept gleaming clean, and can be maintained by just washing with soap and water.

1. *Never* use steel wool or harsh abrasives on modern pewter. The finish will be ruined.

2. Ask any jeweler or silversmith to give you the name of the product recommended by the manufacturer for care of modern pewter.

Iron

IRON, one of the more abundant metallic elements, has been used for implements or ornaments since 1500 B.C., but was known by man long before that date.

Because iron oxidizes readily, the only iron found in a native state is that contained in meteorites. Water and air combined cause iron to rust (that is, to form ferric hydroxide) and left uncontrolled, the whole article will corrode to powder. It is for this reason that relatively few objects made of iron have been successfully excavated after years of burial. Therefore, excavated objects must be handled by experts.

All valuable iron pieces should be cleaned by professionals.

RUST REMOVAL

Patience is needed to remove rust and then control corrosion, for there are several steps to take even in the simplest of methods.

One very knowledgeable craftsman in iron-work suggests the following routine for the removal of rust from such items as hand-rails, garden furniture, and wrought-iron, in general.

1. Using a wire brush or emery, scrape and chip away rust, then sand the area.

2. Cover the cleaned spots with one coat of Manganized-Phospholene .7. This product dissolves any residual rust.

3. Allow to dry completely.

4. Dust off.

5. Next, apply a "zinc rich compound" called Z.R.C.

6. When Z.R.C. is completely dry, paint the article with any good *outdoor* paint. Both the foregoing products are available commercially.

Many products are sold to deter rust; some claim to deter rust and paint the article in one process. They may be excellent but if the rust is not completely removed it will eat through the paint in a few months.

To remove rust from iron ornaments:

1. Dip in kerosene.

2. Rub with fine steel wool.

3. When the kerosene dries, the piece can either be oiled, or painted, as desired.

CARE OF IRON POTS AND SKILLETS

From the earliest times iron pots and skillets were left on the back of the stove to dry and to prevent them from rusting. This is still an excellent plan.

1. Wash iron cooking utensils with any good kitchen soap—liquid is best. Use a kitchen brush to remove food particles.

2. Rinse clean and dry, then place the utensil over low heat on the back of the stove or in a warm oven to complete the drying.

3. If rust spots appear apply salad oil and allow to stand. Remove excess oil before storing. If the rust spot does not disappear when excess oil is wiped away, repeat the process.

If you have several sizes of iron skillets, place paper towels between pans when stacking.

Steel

STEEL is a commerical form of iron and will corrode. To remove rust, use a very fine steel wool such as .0000.

Stainless steel flatware needs only to be washed with soap and water, rinsed and dried. Polishing abrasives are not necessary.

Modern furniture is now being made of ornamental steel. Before attempting any method of cleaning, except dusting, consult with the manufacturer or company from whom you purchased the item.

CARE OF STAINLESS STEEL POTS AND PANS

1. As soon after cooking as possible, soak your pots in soapy water; when you return after the meal, most of the food particles will have loosened, and your cleaning chore will be made easier.

2. There are many excellent stainless steel cleansers available to remove exterior stains.

CARE OF STAINLESS STEEL SINK

1. Clean the sink with any good kitchen scouring powder every few days to prevent stains.

2. Keep the sink wiped dry when not being used.

3. Steel wool is not needed on the steel sinks; it could mark the finish.

Aluminum

ORNAMENTAL aluminum alloys such as candlesticks, salad bowls, dishes, ash-trays, etc. have a lustrous finish that is easily cared for.

1. Mild soap and water will remove finger marks. Rinse and dry.
2. A soft cloth will restore luster.

CARE OF ALUMINUM COOKING UTENSILS

1. Wash aluminum with mild soap and hot water. Fine steel wool or soap pads will not make aluminum gleam.

2. Never use strong soap, or alkaline scouring powders. These alkaline products darken and discolor aluminum.

Alkaline foods or water with high alkaline content also discolor aluminum and can leave a dark surface on the metal.

Remove discoloration by boiling a solution of two teaspoons cream of tartar and one quart of water in the utensil for a few minutes or cook tomatoes in the utensil to remove stain.

To spruce up painted aluminum furniture:

Wear spots and scratches can be hidden by automobile "touch" spray-paint; it is available in almost all colors.

Leather

THE art of treating animal skins to prevent putrefaction and render hides useful, dates too far back into history to trace here, but leather has always been a most important and useful organic material. The tanning of leather is one of man's oldest crafts and has been done by all tribes and cultures from the earliest times.

Most of the leather in common use is made from the hides and skins of domestic animals, cattle being the most important, followed by goatskin, sheepskin, horsehide, and pigskin. The term cattlehide is applied specifically to the hides of full grown steers or cows, as distinguished from calf leathers which, as the name indicates, are the skins of young animals.

American Indians were well versed in leather craft and developed to a high degree the use of leather for clothing, moccasins, and other utilitarian purposes. They further developed the great American art of beading, tooling and fringing of leather.

CARE OF LEATHER

Being organic, leather is easily affected by its environmental climate. Leather becomes dry and brittle in over-heated rooms, and cracks if it is not moisturized and waxed. Proper humidity protects leather bindings, animal skins, fur rugs, etc., and 70° Fahrenheit is the ideal temperature to maintain. If you own fine leather books or leather objects of any value, take care of them—leather, like wood, responds immediately to wax and gentle rubbing.

The following are some of the most popular products used for *waxing, polishing,* and *moisturizing leather:*

Turf Homogenized Cream—leather and saddle soap. Apply as directed on the container.

Lexol—moisturizer for dry, brittle leather. Follow directions on label.

To polish leather apply a thin coat of neutral KiWi; then buff.

For fine articles some authorities recommend Vaseline, sperm oil, or lanolin. Apply *warm,* using soft cloth. Wipe off excess oil; then buff.

Suede

Do not use any of these or comparable products on suede; suede needs special handling. Brushing with a moderately stiff brush will remove finger marks.

Patent leather

Patent leather is easily cared for. Silicon, sprayed on lightly, will remove black scuff marks or superficial stains. Vaseline applied thinly will maintain shine.

SYNTHETIC LEATHERS

These materials are so beautiful that it is often difficult to differentiate the man-made from the real leather. Manufactured in every color of the rainbow, these simulated leather materials are serviceable, easily cleaned, and add a luxurious touch to both interior and exterior decorating when used as upholstery.

These materials are easily cleaned by wiping with a moist cloth. Remove stains as quickly as possible.

SADDLES, BRIDLES, AND OTHER TACK

To clean and maintain the flexibility of leathers, Properts Saddle Soap is an excellent product that can be used daily.

To loosen and remove matted horsehair, mud, and grime, use a sponge moistened in warm water; then rub on a bar of glycerine soap. Remove all residue of soap and dirt with a clean sponge and warm water. To ensure perfection, as the final step rub with a clean stable towel.

For badly damaged dried-out tack, apply Lexol leather conditioner to your now clean surface. I do not recommend neat's foot-oil as it eventually blackens and rots leather. Don't forget to clean bits and stirrups. A toothbrush and metal polish are invaluable for this job. Be sure to rinse carefully.

Papyrus,
Parchment, and Vellum

Down through the ages man has variously used stones, clay, wood, ivory, animal skins, or metals for writing materials. However, the important events of early times were primarily recorded on papyrus, parchment, or vellum.

PAPYRUS

Papyrus, a rush or reed plant grown in the delta of the Nile, was first exploited to make ropes, sails, boats, matting, and cloth. Later, the ancient Egyptians found that it was ideally suited to recording documents and events. From approximately 3000 B.C. to the 9th century A.D., papyrus was used in Egypt as a writing material. The advent of paper eventually supplanted papyrus, parchment, and vellum.

PARCHMENT

Parchment, the second writing material to become popular in ancient times, originated in Pergamon, Asia Minor, in the pre-Christian era. It is made from animal skins and therefore has a stronger surface than papyrus.

Although parchment may be prepared from the skins of various animals, the commonest source is sheepskin. For centuries it has provided the finest grade of writing material for scribes and for illuminators of manuscripts and books. The quality of parchment depends on the dexterity and experience of the craftsman making it. It is interesting to note that there has been little change in the technique of processing parchment throughout the ages.

Because parchment is a hygroscopic, or "moisture sensitive," substance, it will absorb moisture in any amount from its environment. Given the correct relative humidity, parchment tends to absorb or lose moisture in "sympathy" with the rise and fall of the relative humidity of its surroundings.

In an extremely dry atmosphere, in which the relative humidity is at 40% or less, parchment becomes dry and rigid. Its flexibility can be restored, but I advise having any restoration of such valuable materials done by an expert.

Parchment, papyrus, or any animal skins stored in moist, airless spaces develop fungus or mold. Have a professional restorer clean valuable illuminated manuscripts or book bindings—a novice could destroy the colors and the skin.

VELLUM

Vellum, a much finer material than parchment, is made from calfskin. The younger the calf, the finer the vellum. If the calf is over six weeks old, its skin will be too thick for vellum and is sent to the tanner! The most beautiful vellum comes from the stillborn calf. Today, very fine textured paper is referred to as vellum.

Paper

PAPER is organic and, like wood, its fibers expand with moisture and contract when dry. Even though paper might be bound into strong covers, it can be affected by the temperature, humidity, dryness, and polluted air of the environment.

Paper dries and becomes brittle when exposed to $75°$ of heat and a relative humidity of 30 percent—such dry, hot conditions hasten the aging process of paper. Cooler room temperatures with the humidity percentage at 50 retards the aging process.

Dust has a detrimental effect on paper, and should not be allowed to accumulate on unframed prints or books. The sharp edges of dust particles penetrate paper, having a cutting and scouring effect; these particles, once embedded in paper, cannot be removed.

Dust carries micro-organisms that infect paper and these fungus spores thrive in a stagnant, humid environment.

The curative treatment of fungus-infected paper is difficult and demands expert advice. It is a highly specialized field and treatment should never be attempted by the amateur.

Foxing means that brownish freckle-like spots develop on paper under humid conditions if the paper contains iron particles, fungus, or both. The term foxing describes the color of the fox's fur.

PREVENTIVE CARE OF PAPER

Keep valuable paper in controlled, air-conditioned areas.

Paradi-chlorabenzene crystals have a mild fungicidal and insecticidal effect. A few containers of crystals placed on shelves may help.

Beware of paper-destroying insects: silverfish, termites, woodworms, cockroaches, and book-lice. But warn exterminators not to use insecticides that will stain paper, or have adverse effects on *prints* that are to be stored.

Direct exposure to sunlight causes bleaching and deterioration of low quality paper.

Acid Migration is controlled by protective tissues that are placed in new books to prevent the ink of illustrations from transferring to the next page. These tissues turn brown in time and should be discarded, for the ink has long since dried.

FRAMING UNDER GLASS

Framing valuable items under glass requires knowledge, skill and infinite patience. Faulty mounting, matting, and framing has ruined many treasured prints, water-colors, textile pictures or needlework.

1. Glass must be kept well away from the framed picture; temperature changes cause moisture condensation behind the glass, that in turn encourages "foxing" and other serious damage. Museums and collectors now place small *plastic blocks* on the four corners of the mat to lift the glass away from the picture—these blocks are readily available.

2. The backing on any type of picture, framed under glass, must be kept tightly sealed. Torn or loose backing allows penetration of moisture.

3. Old or corroded wiring should be replaced with copper wire, usually preferred by galleries and museums.

4. Loose eye-hooks have been the cause of many an accident. When replacing loose eye-hooks do not use the original hole.

5. To enjoy your pictures, wash the glass occasionally.

CARE OF OIL PAINTINGS

Oil paintings in the home need periodic care because of accumulated dust and dirt from air pollution, plus the drying effect of steam-heat and sunlight. Oil paintings must be cared for by highly skilled experts.

Loose eye-hooks and corroding hanging wire can cause accidents.

1. Use copper wire to replace old wiring.

2. Replace loose eye-hooks in a new hole.

3. Never vacuum oil paintings. The suction could remove the paint from an old, dry canvas.

4. Oil paintings will eventually fade if hung in direct or slanted sunlight.

5. Do not hang paintings over radiators or air-condition vents.

6. Never under any circumstances use a cleaning agent, including soap and water, or any do-it-yourself method. The painting could be ruined. Only an expert should be allowed to clean or varnish an oil painting.

Books

LONG before the printer appeared in history, book binding was an established craft. The earliest books were bound with heavy wooden boards, held together with metal clasps or bands, or with leather lacings. Later, flexible vellum or parchment was used to bind unimportant manuscripts.

In the Middle Ages, monks were the principal book binders; they bound valuable illuminated manuscripts in enamels, ivory, silver and gold, silks and velvets, then lavished time and labor on elaborate designs, built up, element by element, through tooling, inlaying, and embroidering. Extravagant ornamentation with jewels, typical of the Orient, became widespread among these early binders. The art of decorating leather came to Europe from the Arabs, and traces its origin to Coptic techniques of the 6th century A.D.

For hundreds of years animal skins have been used for bindings, and there was a period in Europe when human skin was used.

Cardboard, for binding books, was introduced during the Renaissance by Aldus Manutius, a printer in Venice. This new cover soon replaced the old, heavy, wood bindings, and though significant changes, in both the exterior and interior of books took place in this era, leather and vellum continued to be commonly used. Today leather bindings are very special and very expensive.

CARE OF BOOKS

1. Books need air-circulation; do not over-crowd library shelves. Crowded conditions mar book covers and create other problems.

2. Even though books are vacuum dusted, fine books must be removed from the shelf occasionally to *air the pages*. Ruffling through the leaves removes the musty odor of old paper, and this airing may deter fungus infection, "foxing," or brown spots. If the pages are already covered with brown spots, unfortunately, it's too late; nothing can be done to restore the paper.

3. Never pull a book from the shelf by the top edge of the "spine." Instead, place the fingers onto both sides of the book and carefully remove from the shelf.

4. Forcing open a new book breaks the binding tension and snaps the threads that hold the pages together. If a book is glued, instead of sewn, the pages will fall apart. Open a new book a few pages at a time.

In researching care of books, I note the caution, "do not mark a passage or dog-ear" a page. To me, marking makes a book come alive, and makes the book my private, personal treasure.

When hand-dusting books:

1. Hold the book firmly closed.

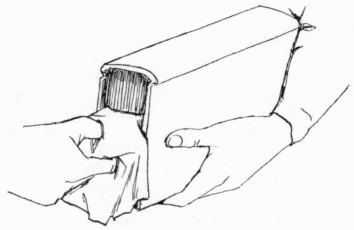

2. Tip the head forward and slanted down with the spine facing up. This handling prevents dust from dropping between pages.

3. Using a treated cloth such as "One-Wipe," is effective when dusting books.

4. "Endust" spread on a clean cloth is also useful.

Gold that is applied to the outer edge of pages seals the edges and prevents dust from sifting between the pages.

For cleaning cloth bindings, the following products are recommended:

1. DemCo Book Cleaner
2. DelKote Bookleen

Use as directed on the label.

CARE OF VALUABLE LEATHER BINDINGS

The care of valuable leather bound books and manuscripts is meticulous work requiring not only skill but scientific knowledge on the curing and tanning of leather, its reaction to chemicals, dryness, humidity and air pollution, plus the reaction of the paper, bound between the covers.

Anyone owning such a collection is already aware of these problems and will have long since been in touch with librarians or museum authorities.

Those of us who have only a few treasured leather bound books or other leather articles can use the two items listed below that are used in well-known libraries. Both products are available commercially from leather or saddle shops and are recommended by the Library Technology Program, American Library Association, Chicago, Illinois. First, vacuum and dust each book; then use as needed the following products, previously noted under Leather:

Turf Homogenized Cream (leather and saddle soap). Apply as directed on the container.

Lexol—moisturizer for dry, brittle leather. Follow directions on label. When this moisturizer dries, one librarian applies a thin coat of neutral KiWi, then buffs to create a polish.

Terry cloth toweling is excellent to use for applying products and is especially good for polishing.

Dr. H. J. Plenderleith, of the British Museum, recommends a dressing from time to time of vaseline, sperm oil, or lanolin, but these oils should be warmed before applying to hasten penetration.

"British Museum Leather Dressing" is commercially available, but is highly inflammable and must be used with care.

SUEDE BINDINGS

Do not use any of these or comparable products on suede bindings, suede needs special handling. Brushing with a moderately stiff brush will remove finger marks.

SYNTHETIC LEATHER BINDINGS

As noted under Synthetic Leathers, these materials are easy to clean. Wipe with a moist cloth. Stains should be removed as quickly as possible.

These books need careful handling or dusting. The leaves are usually glued, not sewn at the "spine." *Rough handling* will cause the leaves to separate from the spine.

To keep from burning your hands or arms when removing pans from oven or burners use potholder *mitts* instead of regular potholders.

Don't leave the dishwasher door open—someone may fall over it and be badly cut.

Don't forget to close cabinet doors and drawers.

Keep the kitchen floor clean. Any small grease spot, ice cube, or liquid spill can result in a bad accident.

Dust, Dirt, and Dullness

Dust and grime that have accumulated on an object over the years or even months is not sacred and does not indicate age or value; it merely shows neglect.

Metals such as silver, gold, copper, brass, and pewter are far from beautiful when they are dull and tarnished. Restoring metals to their original color and lustre may be tedious work, but it can be done and is worth any effort.

Glassware or *crystal* that is dirty loses its sparkle and isn't difficult to clean.

Wood in any form, when neglected, dries, changes color, and shows it needs attention. Caring for wood is probably the most rewarding of all chores because the moment wax is applied, the natural wood color returns and the beauty of the grain is defined; furthermore, the friction created by rubbing the wood gives a mirror-like finish and develops the patina.

This story of neglect covers all categories of furnishings. Look around you—rid your surroundings of dust, dirt, and dullness—you will be delighted to see how quickly inanimate objects and materials respond to care.

HOUSEKEEPING HINTS

Many people believe soap and water are still the most efficient way of removing dirt or dust; this so-called simple method has ruined a lot of things because *wetting* materials in some instances can be destructive. Fine products are available today, formulated to care for specific materials, therefore, and in most instances, replace the old soap-and-water method.

Keep all utensils, brushes, brooms, mops, dust cloths, and polishing cloths clean—vacuum as needed, polish a few items every week and you won't have to tear the rooms apart once a month to have an old fashioned cleaning day!

Hoard old sheets and towels for tearing into cloths. Buy a yard or two of white flannel and cut it into cloths for applying wax and buffing. Very soft sponges are good for applying silver polish.

To keep your home clean the easy way use:

1. A good vacuum cleaner and learn to use each appliance.

2. An electric floor waxer–polisher can be a great help. Teach the family to use it, they might have fun!

3. Don't forget the moth crystals or moth proofing spray.

4. To avoid insect problems keep kitchen drawers and shelves clean.

5. Check various boxes containing oatmeal, corn meal, flour, cereals, crackers, etc. for weevils. There is no cure, discard the food at once.

CLEANING PRODUCTS AND PREPARATIONS

For silver cleaning, I prefer for my own use:

    Hagerty's Silver Foam

    Hagerty's Silver gloves or cloths

    3 M's "Tarni-Shield"

    International Silver Polish.

For Copper, brass, and chrome

    Happich (a German product readily available in this country)

    Twinkle (metal cleaner)

    Revereware (metal cleaner)

    Goddards (metal cleaner)

If nothing else is available for cleaning copper, make a paste of vinegar and flour, rub it on the article, wash and dry.

For waxing furniture

> Partridge's Antiquax (an English product now
> available in the United States)
> Vernax Liquid Furniture Wax and Cleanser
> Goddards Furniture Cream
> Johnson's or Butcher's Floor Paste-wax is an excellent
> substitute for furniture wax

For floor waxing

> Johnson's Floor Paste-wax
> Butcher's Floor Paste-wax

An electric floor waxer-polisher can be a great help. Teach the family to use it; they might have fun!

For waxing leather and leather-bound books

> Lexol (moisturizes)
> Turf Homogenized Cream (leather and saddle soap)
> Neutral Kiwi Wax

Vinegar

Vinegar, one of the oldest products known to man, is still one of the cheapest and most versatile items used in the home. Vinegar flavors, cleans, deodorizes, and preserves food. Three thousand years ago Egyptians used vinegar as a flavoring agent and preservative; they also believed vinegar had medicinal properties. Hippocrates prescribed it for his patients. Roman troops drank vinegar mixed with water—a practice still followed by some peasants who work in the hot sun in southern Europe. During the Civil War vinegar was used for the treatment of scurvy. Currently, the Vinegar Institute figures vinegar production for the United States in 1975 at over 150 million gallons.

> *To make your windows gleam* mix:
> ⅛ cup white vinegar to 1 gal. water;
> wash the glass;
> dry with soft, lintless cloth.

To shine patent leather use a soft cloth moistened with vinegar. Wipe dry.

Rusted or corroded bolts will loosen by soaking in a vinegar bath.

For insect bites, sunburn, hives, and chapped hands, vinegar is a time-honored remedy.

Scouring pads or brushes

The easiest way to handle cooking utensils after removing food is to fill them with hot water and a liquid detergent.

There are various types of scouring pads to clean metal pots and skillets. *Steel soap pads* are essential for maintaining the cleanliness and brightness of metal cooking utensils. Scouring pads made of *copper filaments* are useful but difficult to keep clean. For removing loose food particles from utensils I prefer using an efficient little brush called Lola; you can find it anywhere.

Sponges

Sponges are far from sanitary when used for cleaning pots and pans. Keep sponges for mop-ups and heavy-duty cleaning. Soak frequently in detergent and rinse well, this keeps the sponge clean and useful.

Dishwashing detergents have many uses

To remove baked-on or burned food from ceramicware or metal utensils, put one or more tablespoons of dishwasher detergent in the pan, fill with hot water, and allow to stand several hours or overnight. Food particles will loosen; wash and rinse as usual.

Dishwasher detergent will also remove brown stains and oil of coffee from enamel or ceramic coffeepots. Use one tablespoon dishwashing detergent, fill with hot water, let stand an hour or until stain disappears. Rinse thoroughly with soap and hot water.

Beware of commercial furniture polish sprays

The varnished or lacquered surface on furniture, whether new or antique, can be permanently damaged by the use of commercially advertised quick-polishing sprays that leave an immediate mirrorlike finish. After several applications you will find the wood either sticky or oily and covered with dust that gets harder to remove with each application of the spray. Some furniture sprays include silicon and other materials that are ruinous to the patina or beauty of any wood surface. Don't use these advertised quick-polishing methods. Instead use paste wax two or three times a year, and lots of "elbow grease." Vernax and Goddard's liquid-wax products clean, polish, and protect the wood surface and will in time produce a fine patina.

There are several new products that state there is "no wax in the formula." These sprays, when applied to hard-finished wood surfaces give an immediate shine because the product is oily. Dust disappears as you wipe the surface, then begins at once to collect more dust. Unfortunately, inexperienced housekeepers buy such products not realizing that the tabletops are not being protected from moisture or scratches. These "no-wax" products are a detriment, not a help.

Lemon oil

Never use so-called lemon oil or *any oil product* on hard-finished wood surfaces. All oil collects dust!

There is *no such thing* as *"lemon oil."* Lemon oil, as advertised, is simply a mineral oil, linseed oil, or any oil base scented with the essence of lemon extracted from lemon peel.

THE VACUUM CLEANER

A well functioning vacuum cleaner is the most efficient appliance for removing dust and keeping our possessions clean. Empty the dust bag often; suction stops when the bag is filled with lint and dirt.

Vacuum behind and under overstuffed chairs and sofas. Remove cushions and thoroughly vacuum the seat—you may find a long-last treasure that has fallen behind the cushions.

Carpets, rugs and *floors* must be vacuumed regularly or as often as needed. Vacuum carefully under heavy furniture and in dark areas, these are the favorite breeding grounds for clothes-moths and carpet beetles.

Wall-panelling, door and *window frames* are dirt catchers. Vacuum often to prevent accumulation of dust. Vacuuming can deter the development of mildew.

Lamps and *Light bulbs* are often forgotten. Keep them clean and don't forget to wipe the lightbulbs; it improves their efficiency. Remove any discolored bulbs—they've had it.

Lampshades should be vacuumed or dusted inside and out. Washing and dry-cleaning can be disastrous.

To vacuum venetian blinds

Close the slats, vacuum one side, reverse the slats, and vacuum the second side.

Oil that has accumulated on the slats in oil-heated houses or in kitchens should be removed with ammonia and water or any one of the excellent products formulated for cleaning paint.

Caution: Never remove venetian blinds to immerse them in water. It is a difficult job, unnecessary, and will ruin the cords and tapes. If the cords and tapes are that dirty, broken, or faded, have a venetian blind company clean, re–cord, and retape.

CARE OF SYNTHETIC FLOOR COVERINGS

Before using any *commercial cleaning or waxing product* on man-made synthetic floors, such as vinyl, linoleum, rubber tile, consult with a flooring company. Each type of material demands special cleaning agents or protectives.

Vacuum all floors regularly to remove dirt or grit that might scratch the surface. Kitchens should be vacuumed daily if possible!

Wipe up spills as they occur, quickly mop up coffee stains, alcoholic beverages, and fruit juices with a cloth dipped in mild detergent. Rinse with clear water; dry thoroughly.

To loosen grease, black scuff marks, and heavy stains add one half cup white vinegar or clear household ammonia to one gallon of water.

Damp mop as needed. Washing such floors with soap and water can cause *subsurface rot.* Water seeps through the seams and lies under the flooring; the material loosens, floor boards decay, and the entire room will need reflooring.

Warning:
Scrubbing synthetic flooring with steel wool or any abrasive will destroy the surface finish.
Never use *paste wax* on synthetic flooring.

CARE OF OUTDOOR FURNITURE

To clean the plastic webbing or tubing on outdoor furniture, use soap and water or any commercial product recommended to clean plastic materials. Don't scrub with soap pads or harsh abrasives.

For stubborn stains and mold caused by tree sap or other conditions, make a *thin paste* of clear ammonia and borax. Scrub carefully, using a small utility brush. Rinse with garden-hose and dry.

CARE OF FIREPLACES

1. The fireplace will look nicer if the *fire bricks* are painted black.

Special *fire-brick* paint is available.

2. Check the damper before making or lighting the fire.

3. Have the chimney cleaned and inspected yearly by a professional chimney cleaning company. Many house fires begin in dirty chimneys.

REMOVING PET STAINS

Pet shops have commercial products for removing such stains from carpets but to be effective they must be applied at once; if the stain dries, it will be difficult to remove. Use as directed.

If these products are not available:

As quickly as possible after the spot is discovered, soak the area with club soda. Blot with heavy, absorbent cloth. Repeat process until spot disappears; dry thoroughly.

1. Mix 1 oz. of clear ammonia and 8 oz. of cold water. Soak the area, allow to dry, repeat if stain persists.

2. Do not use soap, it may set the stain.

Recently I found my favorite yellow taffeta curtains had been ruined by dog stains. The dry-cleaning company would not risk cleaning them. Instead, they directed me to their head chemist. He suggested the aforementioned formula be used—at my own risk.

I immersed the soiled area in the ammonia and water. The water became so brown I feared the color had left the fabric. After the material was thoroughly rinsed it was wrapped in terry cloth towels to remove excess water. Discouraged but not willing to give up I ironed the curtains and found all stains were gone. The taffeta was as good as new.

BEWARE OF NEWSPAPER INK

Ink on the newspaper page "comes off" on everything it touches! Look at your hands after you have read the Sunday paper.

Never place newspapers on your carpet, formica counters, marble floors. Any moisture from a bucket filled with water or from a wet sponge or a damp cloth will release the ink and create a real problem. The ink is difficult to remove.

Electrical Equipment

BEFORE using any electrical appliance, study the manufacturer's booklet that comes with the item—full knowledge of an appliance's potentials makes work easier for you and for the machine. Furthermore, expensive "service charges" can be avoided by referring often to the manufacturer's guide and be sure to *unplug* any electric appliance before cleaning.

Remember:

Cut off the electrical switch on any equipment before pulling plug from the wall socket and never pull the plug from the wall socket by its cord. If the switch is "on" when you place the plug in the wall socket you can get a bad shock or blow out the motor in the appliance.

Loose wall sockets are fire hazards and a danger to small children.

Never overload electric outlets or electric extension cords.

T.V., stereo, radio, record players should all be *unplugged* before leaving for vacations; electric leakage can cause fire.

Be sure all T.V.'s, record players, stereos, and radios are *completely* cut-off when through listening to or viewing programs to prevent fire hazard.

Do not tape or try to patch electric cords that are frayed or show wear. *Rewire* the equipment; new wiring is cheap compared to the damage caused by defective wiring.

If heating pads or electric blankets are in any way defective or not heating correctly, throw them out. Don't try repairs.

CARE OF ELECTRICAL APPLIANCES

Keep electrical appliances clean

Can-openers may be hoarding germs. Don't forget to clean the cutting blades.

Toasters need regular care. Open the bottom of the appliance and clean the tray; then use a small brush to dust crumbs off the electric coils.

Blenders and mixers must be thoroughly washed and rinsed after each use.

Refrigerators breed germs unless kept immaculately clean.

To clean: remove food items and wash shelves, walls, doors, and drawers with a solution of:

1 tbsp. of bicarbonate of soda

1 pt. warm water

Rinse with clean water to which bicarbonate of soda has been added. Wash well; wipe with dry cloth.

Caution:

Research has shown that a serious fungus-spore disease can result from stagnant water and slime left too long in the *refrigerator drip-pan.* Once a month remove the drip-pan, wash thoroughly with a strong detergent, rinse with vinegar solution, and dry. Before replacing pan, clean floor under refrigerator.

Do not plug an extension cord into a live socket in the wall and leave the receptacle end unused. A child or animal who chews the open receptacle end can be electrocuted.